Thomas Davies

Dramatic Miscellanies

Consisting of critical observations on several plays of Shakespeare, with a review of his principal characters, and those of various eminent writers, as represented by Mr. Garrick, and other celebrated comedians, with anecdotes

Thomas Davies

Dramatic Miscellanies

Consisting of critical observations on several plays of Shakespeare, with a review of his principal characters, and those of various eminent writers, as represented by Mr. Garrick, and other celebrated comedians, with anecdotes

ISBN/EAN: 9783744748025

Printed in Europe, USA, Canada, Australia, Japan

Cover: Foto ©Thomas Meinert / pixelio.de

More available books at **www.hansebooks.com**

DRAMATIC MISCELLANIES:

CONSISTING OF

CRITICAL OBSERVATIONS

ON SEVERAL

PLAYS OF SHAKSPEARE:

WITH A

REVIEW OF HIS PRINCIPAL CHARACTERS,
AND THOSE OF VARIOUS EMINENT WRITERS,

AS REPRESENTED

By Mr. GARRICK,
AND OTHER CELEBRATED COMEDIANS.

WITH
ANECDOTES OF DRAMATIC POETS, ACTORS, &c.

By THOMAS DAVIES,

AUTHOR of MEMOIRS of the LIFE of

DAVID GARRICK, Esq.

IN THREE VOLUMES.

VOL. II.

DUBLIN:

PRINTED FOR S. PRICE, H. WHITESTONE,
W. WILSON, R. MONCRIEFFE, L. WHITE,
R. MARCHBANK, T. WALKER,
P. BYRNE, R. BURTON,
J CASH, W. SLEATER.

M,DCC,LXXXIV.

DRAMATIC

MISCELLANIES.

All's well that ends well.

CHAPTER XXI.

Unpromising fable to All's well that ends well.—*Shakspeare's creative power.—Revival of this comedy in* 1741.—*Sickness of Milward.—Mrs. Woffington.—Death of Milward.—His character. —Superstition of the actors.—Parolles.—Macklin and* The. Cibber.—*Chapman and Berry commended.—*All's well that ends well *revived by Garrick.—Distribution of the parts.—Abuse of wardship.—Fascinating power of certain worthless characters.—Lully, Swift, and Lord Rivers.* Word Christendom.—*Helen's description of Parolles.—Definition of* clown, *or* fool.—*His occupation.—Description from Johnson and Steevens. —B. Jonson and Fletcher.—Shakspeare's superior knowledge of nature and the qualities of his auditors.—Jonson not averse to mirth in tragedy.— His Sejanus and Catiline.—Condition of physicians in England, France, and Germany.—Helen's delicacy.*

Vol. II.   B   A Phy-

A Physician's daughter curing a king, distempered with a fistula, by a recipe of her dead father, is the history on which this play is founded; a plot strange and unpromising. But the genius of Shakspeare meets with no obstacle from the uncouthness of the materials he works upon. Action and character are the chief engines he employs in this comedy, and he raises abundance of mirth from the situations in which they are placed. Parolles and Lafeu are admirable contrasts, from the collision of whose humours perpetual laughter is produced.

Helen's scheme, of gaining her husband's affections by passing on him for a mistress, has been adopted with success by other dramatists; particularly by Shirley in the Gamester, and Cibber in his first comedy of Love's last Shift.

All's well that ends well, after having lain more than an hundred years undisturbed upon the prompter's shelf, was, in October, 1741, revived at the theatre in Drury-lane. Milward, who acted the King, is said to have caught a distemper which proved fatal to him, by wearing, in this part, a too light and airy suit of clothes, which he put on after his supposed recovery. He felt himself seized with a shivering; and was asked, by one of the players, how he found himself? 'How is it possible for me,' he said, with some pleasantry, ' to be sick, when I have such a physician as Mrs. Woffington?' This elegant and beautiful actress was the Helen of the play.

His distemper, however, increased, and soon after hurried him to his grave.

So pleasing an actor as Milward deserves more than a slight remembrance. In the Memoirs of Garrick's Life, I spoke of him as one who was not without a great share of merit, but was too apt to indulge himself in such an extension of voice as approached to vociferation. He prided himself so much in the harmony and sweetness of his tones, that he was heard to say, in a kind of rapture, after throwing out some passionate speeches in a favourite part, that he wished *he could salute the sweet echo*, meaning his voice. His Lusignan, in Zara, was not much inferior to Mr. Garrick's representation of that part.——Milward chose Booth for his model; and, notwithstanding his inferiority to that accomplished tragedian, he was the only performer in tragedy, who, if he had survived, could have approached to our great Roscius; who, though he would always have been the first, yet, in that case, would not have been the only, actor in tragedy. Milward died about a fortnight after Garrick's first appearance on the stage.

The part of Parolles was, by Fleetwood, the manager, promised to Macklin; but Theophilus Cibber, by some sort of artifice, as common in theatres as in courts, snatched it from him, to his great displeasure. Berry was the Lafeu, and Chapman the Clown and Interpreter. All's well that ends well was termed, by the players, the unfortunate comedy, from the disagreeable accidents which fell out several times during the acting of it. Mrs. Woffington was suddenly taken with illness as she came off the stage from a scene of importance. Mrs. Ridout, a pretty woman and a pleasing actress, after having played Diana one night, was, by the advice of her physician, forbidden to act during a month. Mrs. Butler, in the Countess of Roussillon, was likewise seized with a distemper in the progress of this play.

All's well that ends well, however, had such a degree of merit, and gave so much general satisfaction to the public, that, in spite of the superstition of some of the players, who wished and entreated that it might be discontinued, upon Mr. Delane's undertaking to act the King after Milward's decease, it was again brought forward and applauded.

Cibber's Parolles, notwithstanding his grimace and false spirit, met with encouragement. This actor, though his vivacity was mixed with too much pertness, never offended by flatness and insipidity. Chapman was admirable in the clowns of Shakspeare. Berry's Lafeu was the true portrait of a choleric old man and a humorist. Milward was, in the King, affecting; and Delane, in the same part, respectable.

Under the direction of Mr. Garrick, in 1757, All's well that ends well was again revived. Mrs. Pritchard acted the Countess; Miss Macklin, Helen; Mrs. Davies, Diana. Parolles, Woodward; Lafeu, Berry; and Davies, the King. With the help of a pantomime, it was acted several nights.

Act I. Scene I.

BERTRAM.

I must attend his majesty's command,
To whom I am *in ward*.

No prerogative of the crown, in the time of the feudal system, was esteemed more honourable, or was indeed more profitable, than that of
wardship;

wardship; nor was any part of kingly power more subject to fraudulent abuse, to tyranny and oppression. So cruelly had King John, and some of his predecessors, exerted an undue influence over their wards, that the fourth, fifth, sixth seventh, forty-third, and forty-fourth, articles of the great charter, are all expressly written with an intention to restrain the power of the crown within proper limits respecting wardships.

Helen, after reflecting on Bertram, the object of her love, who had immediately before taken his leave to set out for the court, on seeing Parolles, by her observations on him, prepares the reader for some notable entertainment which is to ensue. Her tenderness in discussing of his vices is a strong, though delicate, confession of her love to Bertram:

HELEN.

——— I love him for his sake;
And yet I know him a notorious liar,
Think him a great way fool, solely a coward:
Yet these fix'd evils sit so fit on him,
That they take place when virtue's steely brows
Look bleak to the cold wind.

There is such a relative charm, in that which in any manner appertains to the person we love, let it be ever so insignificant and worthless, that we are sure to be pleased with it, because it calls to mind the object of our affections. Helen's remark, that the slight and worthless, provided they have talents to excite gaiety and chearfulness, are often preferred to the meritorious, but less pliable in temper, is equally just; and of this many instances can be produced.

Lully,

Lully, the famous French musician, was a debauched fellow and a voluptuary; his company was notwithstanding the delight of all parties, of the witty and the gay, the grave and the learned. He excelled in mimicry and the art of inventing and telling little stories. He was not over nice in the selection of his terms, but indulged a licentious humour to the height. The severe Boileau, who was not so much sought after and invited as Lully, wondered at the distinction bestowed upon that obscene buffoon, as he called him; and would often chide Moliere for his taste in admiring his talent of exciting mirth, for Moliere was as silent in Lully's company as Garrick used to be in Foote's. He was always inviting him to indulge his talent: ' Lully, *fais nous rire*,' Make us laugh,' was the constant address of the great dramatic writer to the merry musician. But this happy talent of pleasing, in a man of merit, and not absolutely abandoned, may be reconciled to conveniency, if not approved by reason. But Parolles was marked with so many vices, that we can hardly justify the countenance given him by his superiors. But there is, in some men, an uncommon power of subduing the minds of others, so that, in spite of a thousand reasons against it, you are so bewitched as not to discern their vices, though ever so gross, through the inchanted veil which they throw over them.

Dr. Swift was, of all men, if we may believe himself, the most cautious in the selection of his friends and companions. Earl Rivers, the father of the unfortunate Savage, was, in Swift's opinion, the most profligate and abandoned of men: and yet he was so inchanted by his irresistible

power

power of pleasing in conversation,* that he could not help declaring, that ' he loved the dog ' dearly.'

The same scene continued.

HELEN.

—————————With a world
Of fond adoptious *Christendoms*.

The word *Christendom* is no where used in this sense by Shakspeare, I believe, except by Prince Arthur, in King John, act iv. scene 1.

——————————By my *Christendom*,
So I were out of prison, and kept sheep,
I should be as merry as the day is long.

Swearing by *Christendom* is swearing by all that is dear.

HELEN.

But the composition that your valour and fear make in you, is the virtue of a good *wing*. I like it well.

Dr. Warburton produces abundance of argument to support his emendations of the text. He would substitute *ming* for *wing*, a word common, he says, in Shakspeare and the writers of the age: ————but where, pray? Dr. Johnson rejects his *ming*, but cannot preserve the original word, *wing*, without allowing it to be a metaphor taken from hawking; and this Mr. Steevens, I think, very substantially proves. Helen's meaning, then,

---

* Amongst other allurements, Homer gives Juno, to charm Jupiter, is the attraction of persuasive conversation.
Παρφασις, η τ' εκλιψε νοον πυκα περ φρονεοντων.
ILIAD. Lib. XIV.

then, may be thus plainly deduced: " The agreement, which is settled between your valour, which is passive, and your fear, which is active, will carry you through all dangers; and you will soar, with a well-poised *wing*, very safely."

HELEN.

The mightiest space in fortune nature brings
To join like likes, and kiss like native things.
Impossible be strange attempts to those
That weigh their pain with sense, and do suppose
What hath been cannot be.

I agree with Dr. Johnson, that these lines are not without obscurity; but our great poet's conceptions were so quick, that he very often did not allow himself time to give them proper clothing. In this passage, Shakspeare gives only the feelings of the character. " There is (says Helen) a certain power in nature to shorten or contract the greatest possible distance that fortune can make between two persons. Let those talk of impossibilities who scrupulously weigh every difficulty from their own cowardly sensations: they do not consider, that what has once happened may again fall out.

Act I. Scene III.

Countess, Steward, and Clown.

The character of Fool, or Clown, was originally introduced into the world to supply the want of that freedom in conversation which was unknown to the savage manners of our ancestors. When half the kingdom was in a state of slavery, under the elder Plantagenets of the Norman race, and

and their immediate successors; when vassalage universally prevailed, and Englishmen were subject to the will of a despotic king, and his haughty and imperious barons; the trade of war was the principal commerce of all the nations in Europe, and tilts and tournaments their great, and almost sole, amusement. The social intercourse, and elegant diversions, which so happily employ both sexes in this refined age, were then utterly unknown; instead of the entertainments of the stage, which we now enjoy in its almost perfect state, the mysteries and moralities of which some specimens are preserved in old writers, were the only theatrical spectacles exhibited from Richard the Second's days to the reign of Queen Elizabeth. Mystery was the tragedy, and morality the comedy: the latter perhaps, owed its origin to the clown or fool, in a motley dress, which every noble family in the kingdom entertained as a necessary appendage of state and grandeur. Nature will insist upon her rights in some shape or other; and mirth is so congenial to man, that it must have a vent. A sarcastic, or perhaps a harmless jest, from one equal to another, in the rough days of the feudal system, would, in all likelihood, have brought about serious consequences, and perhaps ended in a single combat. But kings could not live in their palaces, nor great barons in their castles, without some instrument to excite merriment. They had no wits, indeed, to flatter them; but they had, what men of the most refined understanding love better, a fool to laugh at.

A fellow, dressed in a patched coat, guarded with yellow, was hired, at a certain salary, to divert the great man and his guests. All now was safe; for nobody could pretend to be angry with the sarcastic gibes or saucy petulancies of a party-coloured hireling; one too, who was himself the butt of the company. The fool treated all alike; the master and his guests were equally the objects of his satirical mirth; and I make no doubt that a keen-witted fellow would sometimes revenge the disgrace of situation on his betters, by uttering severe reproach and home truth under the cover of a joke, which no man durst resent without being exposed to the derision of the company.

Viola, in Twelfth Night, aptly describes the business of a fool by profession:

> This fellow is wise enough to play the fool,
> And to do that well craves a kind of wit.
> He must observe their mood on whom he jests,
> The quality of the persons, and the time;
> And, like the haggard, check at every feather
> That comes before his eye.——

Riccoboni, in his history of the Italian theatre, deduces the Harlequin and Scapin from the Roman Sannio: " For the Sannio is nothing else, he says, but our buffoon." To support his hypothesis, he alleges the authority of Cicero, in his book De Oratore : '*Quid enim potest tam ridiculum quam Sannio esse? Qui ore, vultu, imitandis motibus, voce, denique corpore, ridetur ipso.*'

Barrett, in his Alvearie, seems to be of the same opinion with respect to the Sannio, or fool, as Riccoboni, " *The vice, or gestor, began the dance.—Sannio saltationem occepit.*"

None of our old dramatic writers have made such frequent and happy use of this character as Shakspeare. The immediate predecessor of his

clown

clown he found in The Moralities, which never were without a fellow dressed in a long coat, a cap on his head with a pair of asses ears, and a dagger of lath * by his side. The sport between him and his adversary, the devil, was a perpetual source of mirth and loud laughter.

Ben Jonson, and his friends Beaumont and Fletcher, very seldom employed this merry agent in their plays. Their classical learning placed them, it is thought, above the use of so mean an instrument. It may be so: but, I believe, their pieces did not succeed the better for their contempt of the public taste. The stage was then in its infancy, nor could the people, all at once be weaned from their baubles, their caps and bells, and party-coloured liveries.

Shakspeare, who understood human nature better than Jonson and his admirers, was resolved not to resign an engine of which he could make so notable an use. He had taken full measure of the understanding, humour, and taste, of his audience; and no physician was ever more accurately acquainted with the pulse of his patient than our poet was with the peculiar diet which would please the palates of the good folks in this metropolis. After a serious, or pathetic, scene, he knew that his clown would revive the mirth, cheer the spirits, and dry the tears, of his auditors. And, I know not, after all, if the man, who can excite our mirth, and command our grief, successively, may not be the best dramatic cook to prepare entertainment for a people so melancholy and so merry, so sprightly and so sad, as the English are generally said to be.

So

---

* Johnson and Steevens's Shakspeare.

So convinced was Shakſpeare that his countrymen could not be ſatisfied with their dramatic exhibitions without ſome mixture of merriment, that, in his moſt ſerious plays, he has thrown in characters of levity, or oddity, to enliven the ſcene. In King John we have the baſtard Falconbridge; in Macbeth, the witches; who, tho' not abſolutely comic, never fail to provoke laughter. In Julius Cæſar, Caſca and the mob; in Hamlet, Polonius, the grave diggers, and Oſtrick; nay, in Othello, his laſt and moſt finiſhed tragedy, beſides a happily-conceived drunken ſcene of Caſſio, we are preſented with the follies of a Roderigo: theſe comic characters, placed in proper ſituations to produce action ariſing from the plot, never failed to raiſe gaiety and diverſion amidſt ſcenes of the moſt affecting pathos and the moſt afflicting terror. What affords the moſt evident proofs of our author's infallible judgment and ſagacity is, that, notwithſtanding the great alteration and improvement in the public taſte, reſpecting the amuſements of the theatre, theſe characters and ſcenes never fail to produce the ſame effect at this day; and who, after all, is offended with the idle politics and ſilly pedantry of Polonius, after admiring the wonderful interview of Hamlet and the ghoſt! Who does not laugh at the prattling and goſſipries of the nurſe, when Juliet has taken a ſad and mournful leave of her beloved Romeo?

Ben Jonſon was not averſe to the uſe of the characters and language of comedy in his tragedies; but Ben underſtood not the art of blending them ſo happily as not to deſtroy the effect of either. In his Sejanus, he introduces a ſcene between the principal character of the play and
Eudemus

ALL'S WELL THAT ENDS WELL. 15

Eudemus the physician. Sejanus gravely interrogates the doctor concerning the effect of the physic he administers to the ladies, his patients, and is anxious to know which of them, during the operation, made the most wry faces: this is below farce.—Nay, so lost is this learned author to all sense of decency and decorum, that Catiline, in the grand scene of conspirators, in Act III. threatens one of his young associates with the severest punishment for his reluctance to submit to the most infamous of all crimes!

The scene continued.

CLOWN.

I shall never have the blessing of God till I have issue of my body; for, they say, bearns are blessings.

The Clown's opinion corresponds with that of all mankind, and more particularly with the Jews. They hold barrenness to be a great curse. No people in the world multiply so fast as they. Sir James Porter, in his letters on the Turkish nation, after informing us that, by a certain law in the Alcoràn, when no heirs male are left in the family the estate is immediately forfeited to the emperor, assures his readers it is next to a miracle to hear of the effects of a Jewish family being forfeited to the Sultan for want of heirs.

COUNTESS.

The mystery of your loveliness————

Which, I think, a happy emendation of Theobald from *loveliness*.

Mr.

Mr. Tyrrwhit prefers, instead of *loneliness*, a suggestion of Mr. Hall in favour of *lowliness*; but Mr Steevens seems to understand the language of love better than his friend, and justifies Theobald. If Mr. Tyrrwhit wants an authority for a person in love being fond of retirement and solitude, Romeo and Juliet will give him one. Romeo, Act I.

MONTAGUE.

Away from light steals home my giddy son,
And private in the chamber pens himself.

And Rosalind, in As you like it, when she can no longer enjoy the company of Orlando, leaves her cousin Cælia to find a shadow and to sleep.

HELEN.

My friends were poor, but honest; so is my love!

Helen pleads that, although she is no higher in rank than a physician's daughter, yet her love is as much mark'd for sincerity as her relations were esteemed for their integrity.

In no part of Europe is the worth of a learned and skilful physician so well understood, and so generously rewarded, as in England. In France, till very lately, physicians were placed in a lower class. The ancients, in the opinion of Dr. Middleton, who wrote a Treatise *de Conditione Medicorum apud Antiquos*, rated them not much higher than slaves. In Flanders, the customary fee, to a physician, is no more than half a crown: I believe it is the same through Holland and all Germany.

But

But Helen's love is as honeſt as her parentage. It appears, throughout the whole play, that the paſſion of this ſweet girl is of the nobleſt kind: ' Nature, ſays Shakſpeare, in Hamlet, is fine in love;' that is, it purifies and refines our paſſions. Before marriage Helen diminiſhes the blemiſhes of Parolles, becauſe he is the conſtant companion of Bertram, and after marriage; tho' ſhe might reaſonably exclaim againſt the ſeducer of her huſband, with the utmoſt delicacy ſhe reſtrains herſelf from the leaſt reproach: nay, converts a queſtion, implying cenſure, to a mark of honour.

CHAP.

CHAP. XXII.

Meaning of Good faith acrofs.—*Helen's tax of impudence, &c.—Theobald defended.—Several paffages explained.—A fcene of Parolles.—His character.—Compared with that of Beffus.—King and no King intended to have been revived by Mr. Garrick.—Why thrown afide.—Inceft an improper fubject for a play.—Don Sebaftian.—Maffinger's unnatural combat.—Beffus a pander as well as a coward.—Cowardice in the abftract.—No proper fubject of mirth.—Parolles admirable to the laft.—Time and Dr. Johnson.—Helen's ring.—Queen Elizabeth and the Earl of Effex.*

Act. II. Scene I. King and Lafeu.

LAFEU.

Pardon, my lord, for me and for my tidings.

KING.

I'll fee thee to ftand up.

LAFEU.

——————— Then here's a man
Stands that has bought his pardon. I would you
Had kneel'd, my lord, to afk me mercy; and
That at my bidding you could fo ftand up.

KING.

I would I had, fo I had broke thy pate,
And afk'd thee mercy for it.

LAFEU.

——————Good faith, acrofs.

ALL'S WELL THAT ENDS WELL. 19

IT was neceſſary to quote theſe ſeveral ſpeeches that the ſenſe of the laſt words might be better underſtood. Dr. Johnſon interprets the expreſſion, ' a croſs,' to mean, a paſs in wit that miſcarries. I think quite otherwiſe. The King, not being, through infirmity, able to raiſe Lafeu from kneeling, ſays he will ' ſee him to ſtand up.' Lafeu wiſhes that the King, even on the humiliating condition of aſking pardon of him, his ſubject, could ſtand as firmly. ' So would I,' replied the King, ' though I had broken your pate at the ſame time, and aſked your pardon for it.' The anſwer, of ' Good faith, acroſs,' is as much as to ſay, ' With all my heart, ſir, though you had broken my head acroſs;' which, in the language of thoſe days, ſignified a very ſevere blow or contuſion on the head. Twelfth Night, act v. ſcene 5. Sir Andrew Aguecheek. ' *He has broke my head acroſs*, and given Sir Toby a bloody coxcomb too.'

KING.

Thus he his ſpecial nothing ever prologues.

So, in the Merchant of Venice, Antonio characteriſes Gratiano:

Gratiano ſpeaks an infinite deal of nothing.

KING.

Upon thy certainty and confidence
What dareſt thou venture?

HELEN.

HELEN.

———— ———— Tax of impudence,
A Strumpet's boldness, a divulged shame,
Traduc'd by odious ballads; my maiden's name
Sear'd otherwise; no worse of worse extended,
With vilest tortures let my life be ended.

Mr. Steevens, in his very ingenious note upon this obscure passage, has not, I think, cleared all the difficulties of it.——He imagines that Helen, in her covenant with the King, to suffer all manner of indignities if she does not perform the promised cure, excepts the violation of her chastity. But she is so confident of success, that she does not imagine a possibility of failure; besides, the infamous violation of a virgin, or woman, has been no part of the penal laws in Christian Europe, though it certainly was the practice in old Rome, and especially during the emperors. If we attend a little to the mode of expression, we may fairly conclude, that Helen, by ' no worse of worst extended,' meant, that the branding her maiden character with the name of a whore was the worst punishment that could be extended to her.

Scene the third.

LAFEU.

We make trifles of terrors, ensconcing ourselves into seeming knowledge, when we should submit ourselves to an unknown fear.

Our author, in several of his plays, ridicules the philosophers of the times in which he lived, who endeavoured to account for all uncommon appearances in nature, either by attributing them

to

to the agency of second causes, or to some principle still more bold and uncertain: whereas Shakspeare insinuates, that it would be more modest to confess our ignorance, in things beyond our capacities to comprehend, and attribute their existence to some cause unknown to us.

KING.

——— ——— Good alone
Is good without a name. Vileness is so.

That is, 'if vice be detestable, as it certainly is, from its intrinsic baseness; so must virtue be, from its own purity, without the help of any addition whatsoever.'

I believe Mr. Steevens, whom nothing escapes, is rather beforehand with me in this explanation, or at least in something very near it.

KING.

My honour's at the stake; which to *defeat*,
I must produce my power.

Mr. Theobald, who was not well pleased with his exaltation to the throne of dulness, embraces every opportunity to turn into ridicule Pope's emendations of Shakspeare; he laughs at the word *defeat*, and terms it nonsensical; he proposes to substitute the word *defend* in its room. Dr. Farmer candidly and ingeniously supposes, that Mr. Theobald was not aware that the clause of the sentence served for the antecedent. Mr. Tyrrwhit very improperly taxes Theobald with pertness; he recommends the old reading, and fortifies it from an explanation of the French verb *défaire*. I must confess that Theobald's *defend* answers the purpose of the reader and auditor

much

much better than the old word *defeat*, which cannot be maintained without much subtlety of argument. However the critics may determine, I would advise the actor to retain *defend*, as more intelligible to an audience.

LAFEU.

I think thou waſt created for men to breath themſelves upon.

Lafeu is not very nice in the choice of terms to expreſs his ſcorn and contempt of Parolles. 'Breathe upon' is to be underſtood in the ſame ſenſe as a ſpeech of Prince Henry to Poins, concerning the tavern-waiters, act 2d of Henry IV. Firſt Part:

And when you breathe in your watering, they cry hem! and bid you play it off.

Act III. Scene V.

HELEN.

I thank you, and will wait upon your leaſure.

An uſual phraſe of civility in Shakſpeare's time, and explains a paſſage in Hamlet, act the 3d:

The players wait upon your patience

Act IV. Scene II.

DIANA.

'Tis not the many oaths that make the truth,
But the plain ſimple vow that is vow'd true.
What is not holy, that we ſwear not by,
But take the High'ſt to witneſs; then, pray you, tell me,
If I ſhould ſwear by Jove's great attributes, &c.

In the explanation of these lines, much has been said by the commentators. Mr. Steevens has, from the revisal, judiciously supported the text. Perhaps a short interpretation of Diana's intention may satisfy the common reader better than a more learned discussion:

'The multitude of oaths prove nothing. That vow alone is valuable which is founded on truth and sanctified by religion. Could you possibly believe me, though I should appeal to heaven for the truth of what I uttered, when, at the same time, I was acting against my honour and my conscience?'

DIANA.

Since Frenchmen are so *braid*.

The word *braid*, I believe, means *practised*, *accustomed*, or *beaten to a thing.*——'Bray a fool in a mortar.'

BERTRAM.

By an *abstract* of Success.

That is, 'by an *abstract*, or *memorandum*, of what I have taken down successively in order.' So, in the Merry Wives of Windsor, Mrs. Ford tells Falstaff, who wants to hide himself in her apartment, that her husband keeps an *abstract* of every thing that is in that chamber.

IDEM.

The business is not done, as fearing to hear of it hereafter.

Bertram means his intrigue with Diana. 'If the consequence of our meeting should be a child,

child, I may chance to be called upon to maintain it.'

IDEM.

Entertained my convoy.

'Made a bargain with the men who are to attend me in my journey, and take care of my baggage, &c.'

BERTRAM.

I con him no thanks for this.

'Con him' is a Scottish phrase, and still in use.

IDEM.

He is a cat still.

Bertram calls him a *cat* three times, as a mark of great and incurable aversion. All his phrases of that kind are to be understood as in the Jew's list of antipathies in the Merchant of Venice:

Some that are mad if they behold a cat.

PAROLLES.

He will steal eggs out of a cloister.

This has the same meaning as to 'rob the 'spital.'

IDEM.

Faith, Sir, he has led the drum before the English tragedians.

It

It was formerly customary with the English itinerant players, and perhaps peculiar to them, to announce the play by beat of drum, and at the same time to distribute bills of the play to the populace.

PAROLLES, SOLUS.

Yet am I thankful. If my heart were great,
'Twould burst at this. Captain I'll be no more.

This scene always afforded much pleasure to the audience. Upon its last revival, it was acted with such theatrical skill as excited general meriment. The unbinding Parolles, who looked about him with anxious surprize and terror, redoubled the bursts of laughter which echoed round the theatre. Woodward was excellent in the whole scene, but particularly in characterizing Bertram and the Dumaines, whose feelings, upon the unexpected heap of slander which he threw upon them, served to heighten the scene. Bertram was most angry, because Parolles deviated very little from the truth in what he said of him; his lasciviousness, and his intrigue with Diana, he could not deny.

In all our comic writers, I know not where to meet with such an odd compound of cowardice, folly, ignorance, pertness, and effrontery, with certain semblances of courage, sense, knowledge, adroitness, and wit, as Parolles. He is, I think, inferior only to the great master of stage gaiety and mirth, Sir John Falstaff.

Bessus, in the King and no King of Beaumont and Fletcher, is, I know, highly extolled, as a great original, by some writers; and particularly by Mr. Seward, a very able commentator upon

Beaumont

Beaumont and Fletcher, as a character second only to the inimitable Fat Knight.

That Beſſus might, in his own days, be eſteemed as a juſt portrait of an impudent boaſter and a blaſted coward, and one who profeſſed to fight according to the rules of Caranza and Saviolino, thoſe great adepts in the art of challenging and fighting, I ſhall not deny; but this I will venture to ſay, that he is ſo widely different from any character we ſee at preſent, that no comic poet of this age will undertake his revival, even with conſiderable alterations; he is ſo outrageouſly diſtorted, in every limb and feature, that nothing but a new creation will do for Beſſus.

Soon after his preſent majeſty's acceſſion, Mr. Garrick intended to have brought forward to the public the King and no King of Beaumont and Fletcher. Beſſus was given to Woodward; the manager deſigned Arbaces for himſelf. They both appeared to be much pleaſed with the proſpect of giving the public diverſion, and gaining great applauſe in the repreſentation of two characters new to the ſtage. And, doubtleſs, the quick tranſitions, from ſudden anger and violent rage to calm repentance and tame ſubmiſſion, in Arbaces, could not have been diſplayed with equal ſkill by any actor but Garrick; though a character, which is all paſſion and all repentance, is like a picture without keeping: the light and ſhade, though ſtrong, receive no advantage from the perſpective: the diſtreſs of Arbaces is, from ſituation, continually bordering upon the ridiculous.

The abſurdity, baſeneſs, and cowardice of Beſſus, could not have been better diſpoſed of,

perhaps,

perhaps, than to Harry Woodward. The other parts were distributed to advantage; the play was curtailed of such scenes as were supposed to be superfluous, and in some places altered and improved. But, however eager the manager was to bring out this play at first, it was observed, that, at every reading of it in the green-room, his pleasure, instead of increasing, suffered a visible diminution. His usual vivacity at last forsook him; he looked grave and stroked his chin, which, to the courtiers amongst the players, who knew their monarch was his own minister, was a convincing sign of his being dissatisfied with the business that was going forward. At length he fairly gave up the design of acting King and no King; the parts were withdrawn from the actors, and no more was heard of it.

The cause of this sudden resolution was not known, though the conjectures concerning it were various. Some thought the title carried an objection. The words, King and no King, they said, would make an odd appearance in the bills, more especially as a young and beloved prince had just ascended the throne of his ancestors. Others thought the impropriety of the story, on which the play was founded, was a great defect; but this objection could have small weight, as the plots of almost all our old dramatists are built upon romances, or histories of very little credit.

Two reasons, above all others, I believe, prevailed on the manager to drop this play. The King's strange and contradictory agitations of mind are no otherwise to be accounted for than from his ardent passion to a lady whom he supposes to be his sister: this belief raises him sometimes to fits of frenzy. A play, founded upon incest, or any thing repugnant to nature, even in supposition, can never please an English audience. ——Why is Dryden's Don Sebastian almost banished our theatres? The progress of the play, to a glorious fourth act, promises a noble catastrophe. In the fifth act, the two lovers, Sebastian and Almeyda, are discovered to be brother and sister. After exchanging amorous glances and warm wishes, approaching to lasciviousness, in the rich eloquence of Dryden's harmonious verses, they are obliged to part for ever. The Unnatural Combat of Massinger, one of his most finished pieces, is for ever excluded the theatre for a like reason. Smith's Phædra and Hippolitus was coldly entertained, at the first acting of it, with all the powers of Betterton and Booth, Barry and Oldfield, to support it; and could never win upon an audience in a revival.

But another very powerful reason for not acting King and no King prevailed, I am persuaded, with a man of Garrick's reflection. He did not choose to hazard the obtruding such a character on the public as Bessus, who, though a captain in the army, is not only a beaten and disgraced coward, but a voluntary pandar; a wretch who offers to procure a lady for the king his master, supposed, by him, to be his own sister; and, not satisfied with this degree of infamy, by way of supererogation, he declares he would not scruple to go on the same scandalous errand to the king's mother. This fellow is a rare second to Jack Falstaff, for so we are informed in the animated lines of Mr. Colman to Philaster:

Beaumont

Beaumont and Fletcher, those twin stars that run
Their glorious course round Shakspeare's golden sun;
Or when Philaster Hamlet's place supply'd,
Or Bessus walk'd with Falstaff by his side.

As cowardice, in the abstract, is a bad subject of ridicule, so is the wretch who is employed to raise the mirth of an audience by being often kicked. Can we laugh at him, who, when completely drubbed says, ‘ That sufferance has made ‘ me wainscot.’

Humanity must be shocked at this as well as what follows: ‘ *There is not a rib in his body that has not been thrice broken with dry beating, and now his sides look like two wicker targets, every way bended.*’ King and no King. Act IV.

This may be wit, but it is of the bluntest sort I ever met with; but, as if this was not sufficient, after the theatre has echoed with the mirth resulting from the two severe drubbings of this second Falstaff, in a subsequent scene he is twinged by the nose, kicked, beaten, and trod upon.

What must we think of an audience that could be diverted with such hyperbolical stuff, and such cruel treatment of a poor miserable wretch, after having been delighted with the truly diverting scenes of a Parolles and a Falstaff? This surely is being

‘ Sated with celestial food, and feeding upon garbage.’

It is more to be wondered Mr. Garrick could have any thoughts of reviving King and no King, than that he should afterwards withdraw it.

It has been said that Mr. Garrick had once made a promise to a gentleman, respectable for elegance of taste and politeness of manners, to act Arbaces and Bessus alternately. This promise must

must have been made when Roscius was in a very gay humour; or, at least, much off his guard.

The cowards of Shakspeare are not rendered so absolutely unfit for all society as Bessus and his companions, the swordsmen; fellows who gravely take measure of a man's shoe to discover by that whether the owner had kicked a fellow into disgrace or not. Though we should grant that Parolles, in real life, would not be a very eligible companion, yet, I believe, no audience would refuse his acquaintance. Beaumont and Fletcher place their cowards in such situations as must produce nothing but contempt and disgust. Parolles fetches out rich matter, fine spleen, and choleric humour, from old Lafeu. His distress, when blinded, is of the most whimsical sort, and the acute invention of his answers, to the interpreter's interrogatories, afford perpetual laughter.

Even, in his last stage of Tom Drum, when he is produced as an evidence against Bertram, the rogue is so characteristically diverting that you cannot find in your heart to be very angry; you almost pardon him, and wish he were taken into favour again. The generous Lafeu is half inclined to it, and, that he is made so relenting, we must attribute to our author's great knowledge of man and *his large nature,* as Ben Johnson expresses it. He knew that those who are most prone to vehement anger are the soonest pacified. Hot spirits make quicker haste to repair the mischiefs of their escapes from reason, than those who are more temperate and sedate.

Act V. Scene III.

KING.

For we are old, and, on our quickest decrees,
The inaudible and noiseless foot of time
Steals ere we can effect them.

Dr. Johnson, in his life of Pope, has an excellent thought on the unconquerable power of time: 'He that runs against time has an antagonist not subject to casualties.'

IDEM.

This ring was mine, and, when I gave it Helen,
I bade her, if her fortune ever stood
Necessitated to help, that, by this token,
I would relieve her.—————

This is so like the circumstance of Queen Elizabeth's giving a ring to the Earl of Essex, with the same kind intention, in behalf of that unfortunate nobleman, that I cannot help thinking that our author inserted it, in his play, from that well-known fact. I am aware that All's well that ends well was first acted in 1598, though not printed till 1623: but our author, it is known, frequently made alterations and additions to several of his pieces.

LAFEU.

I will buy me a son-in-law in a fair, and toll for this.

'I will rather go to a country fair, where I shall have my choice of peasants or country clowns, and pick out a son from them, than marry my daughter to so worthless a fellow as this, whose knell I would most willingly ring.' I do not presume to give this as the infallible meaning of the passage in question; but it is surely very probable.

BERTRAM.

[*Speaking of Parolles.*]———What of him?
He's *quoted* for a most perfidious slave,
With all the spots o'th' world tax'd and debosh'd.

Mr. Steevens says, rightly, that *quoted* has the same sense as *noted*; but, in this particular place, it bears, I think, a yet stronger meaning. ' He is stigmatised as a well-known and most abhorred liar."

King John's reproach to Hubert contains a fuller interpretation of this word than Polonius's ' quoted him,' in Hamlet:

———————Hadst not thou been by,
A fellow, by the hand of nature mark'd,
Quoted, and sign'd to do a deed of shame,—&c.

Every Man in his Humour.

CHAPTER XXIII.

Particular merit of Every Man in his Humour.—*Ben Jonson's language—Kitely and Bobadil.—Master Stephen and Slender.—Clement, Downright, and Brainworm.—Knowell.—Anecdote of Shakspeare and Jonson.—Prologue to* Every man in his Humour.—*Jonson's malice.—Dennis's thunder.—This comedy revived after the Restoration.—Account of its revival.—Lord Dorset's prologue.—Mistake of Downs.—Medbourne and the popish plot.—*Every Man in his Humour *revived by Garrick.—Merit of the several actors.—Some account of the dead and living.—Anecdote of Garrick and Woodward.—Mrs. Ward, Delane, and Garrick.—Messieurs Smith, Palmer, Dodd, and Baddeley, commended.—Henderson.—*Every man out of his humour. — *Dr. Hurd and Carlo Buffone.—Definition of humour.—Jonson's panegyric of Queen Elizabeth.—His poetaster.—Quarrel with the players.—Whom he satirises.—Conjectures concerning them.*

EVERY Man in his Humour is founded on such follies and passions as are perpetually incident to, and connected with, man's nature; such as do not depend upon local custom or change of fashion; and, for that reason, will bid fair to last as long as many of our old comedies. The language of Jonson is very peculiar; in perspicuity and elegance he is inferior to Beaumont and Fletcher, and very unlike the masculine dialogue of Massinger. It is almost needless to observe that he comes far short of the variety, strength, and natural flow, of Shakspeare. To avoid the common idiom, he plunges into stiff, quaint, and harsh, phraseology: he has borrowed more words, from the Latin tongue, than all the authors of his time. However, the style of this play, as well as that of the Alchemist and Silent Woman, is more disentangled and free from foreign auxiliaries than the greatest part of his works. Most of the characters are truly dramatic: Kitely, though not equal to Ford in The Merry Wives of Windsor, who can plead a more justifiable cause of jealousy, is yet well conceived, and is placed so artfully in situation, as to draw forth a considerable share of comic distress.

Bobadil is an original. The coward, assuming the dignity of calm courage, was, I believe, new to our stage; at least, I can remember nothing like him. From Bobadil, Congreve formed his Noll Bluff; a part most admirably acted by Ben Jonson the comedian. Master Stephen is an honester object of ridicule than Master Slender. One is nature's oaf, consequently rather an object of compassion than scorn. The other is a fop of fashion, and the imitator of the follies which he admires in his companions. Clément and Downright are strongly marked with humour, especially the first; and Brainworm is a fellow of merry and arch contrivance. In drawing this character, I believe the author had Terence, or rather, Plautus, of whom he was acknowledged to be an imitator, in his eye. Wellbred and
young

young Knowell are diſtinguiſhed by no peculiarities. Old Knowell is ſomething like the anxious Simo of Terence.

A remarkable anecdote, concerning the introduction of this play to the theatre, has been handed down traditionally. Ben Jonſon preſented his Every Man in his Humour to one of the leading players in that company of which Shakſpeare was a member. After caſting his eye over it careleſsly and ſuperciliouſly, the comedian was on the point of returning it to the author with a peremptory refuſal; when Shakſpeare, who perhaps had never, till that inſtant, ſeen Jonſon, deſired he might look into the play. He was ſo well pleaſed with it, on peruſal, that he recommended the work and the author to his fellows. The ſucceſs of the comedy was conſiderable, and we find that the principal actors were employed in it; Burbage, Kempe, Hemmings, Condell, and Sly. Shakſpeare himſelf is generally ſaid, by his name being firſt in the drama, to have acted the part of Old Knowell. He was, at that time, in the thirty-fourth year of his age, and Ben Jonſon in his twenty-fourth.

Notwithſtanding the friendſhip which Shakſpeare had manifeſted to Ben, by patronizing his play, yet the reader will find that the prologue is nothing leſs than a ſatirical picture of ſeveral of Shakſpeare's dramas, particularly his Henry V. and the three parts of Henry VI. I am of opinion, too, that Lear and the Tempeſt are pointed at in the following lines:

> Nor creaking throne comes down the boys to pleafe,
> Nor nimble fquib is feen to make afeard
> The gentlewomen, nor roll'd bullet heard
> To fay it thunders, nor tempeftuous drum
> Rumbles to tell you when the ftorm is come.

Thefe lines may indeed apply, as the editor of Jonfon hinted to me, to other writers as well as Shakfpeare; but, as they follow other lines, unqueftionably hoftile to him, I cannot avoid believing that he levelled the whole principally at the man whom he moft envied.

The playhoufe thunder was compofed of much the fame materials in Queen Befs's days as in the reign of George III. I never heard of any improvement in the theatrical artillery of the fky, if we except that fort of which Mr. Dennis claimed the invention; but whether he mixed any particular ingredients in the bullet, or ordered that a greater number of them fhould be rolled in a particular direction, or whether he contrived a more capacious thunder-bowl, I am really at a lofs for information; but fo jealous was he left his art of making thunder fhould be imparted to others, without his confent, that Mr. Pope informs us, he cried out vehemently, at fome tragedy, upon hearing an uncommon burft of thunder, " By G— that's my thunder." Whether the fame critic invented the reprefentation of heavy fhowers of theatrical rain, by rattling a vaft quantity of peas in rollers, I am equally ignorant.

Every

Every Man in his Humour was first published in 1602. The prologue was not added to that edition of the play, nor must we suppose that it was spoken originally; and indeed, such a gross affront to their great friend would not have been permitted by the players. I do not think that this insolent invective was ever pronounced on the stage, nor printed, till after the death of Shakspeare, who died in April, 1616, which, according to the then reckoning of time, was soon after the beginning of the year. Jonson collected his works into one volume in the same year, and took that opportunity of indulging his posthumous malice, by fixing this introduction to his first play. This is of a piece with his general conduct through his whole life to Shakspeare. When he sat down to write a panegyric *on his beloved*, prefixed to his works, as he there calls Shakespeare, he must, for a time, have purged his brain and heart of all spleen, envy, and malevolence: for a more accurate or extensive eulogium, on the genius and writings of Shakspeare, could not well be conceived.

Amongst the old plays revived, upon the opening of the theatres after the Restoration, this comedy was not forgotten. It was acted, as I conjecture, about the year 1675, by the Duke of York's company, in Dorset Gardens. Not having met with a printed copy of the play, as then acted, I cannot easily divine how the parts were divided. In all probability, Betterton, Smith, Harris, Nokes, Underhill, and some others of the prime comedians, were employed in it.

A taste

A taste for Jonson was endeavoured to be revived: though, I believe, that was always an up hill work; and in this belief I am confirmed from some shrewd reflections thrown out by L. Diggs, in a copy of verses prefixed to Shakspeare's poems. However, the recommendation was so powerful, that it amounted to a command. The Earl of Dorset favoured the players with an epilogue, from which we learn that the parts were well fitted. It contains some stage anecdotes or history which may not be displeasing to the readers, more especially as Lord Dorset's works, separately printed, are not to be met with.

Epilogue on the revival of Ben Jonson's play, called, Every Man in his Humour.

[*The actor is supposed to enter with reluctance.*]

Intreaty shall not serve, nor violence,
To make me speak in such a play's defence.
A play, where wit and humour do agree
To break all practis'd laws of comedy.
The scene, what more absurd L in England lies:
No gods descend; no dancing devils rise;
No captive prince from unknown country brought;
No battle; nay, there's scarce a duel fought.
And something yet more sharply might be said,
But I consider, the poor author's dead;
Let that be his excuse,——now for our own:
Why,——faith, in my opinion, we need none.
The parts were fitted well; but some will say
Pox on them, rogues! what made them take this play?

I do

I do not doubt but you will credit me;
It was not choice, but mere neceffity.
To all our writing friends in town we fent,
But not a wit durft venture out in Lent:
Have patience but till Eafter Term, and then
You fhall have jog and hobby-horfe again.
Here's Mafter Matthew, our domeftic wit,
Does promife one o' th' ten plays he has writ.
But, fince great bribes weigh nothing with the juft,
Know we have merits, and to them we truft.
When any fafts or holidays defer
The public labours of the theatre,
We ride not forth, altho' the day be fair,
On ambling tit, to take the fuburb air;
But with our authors meet, and fpend that time
To make up quarrels between fenfe and rhyme.
Wednefdays and Fridays conftantly we fat;
Till, after many a long and free debate,
For divers weighty reafons, 'twas thought fit,
Unruly fenfe fhould ftill to rhyme fubmit.
This the moft glorious law we ever made,
So ftrictly in this epilogue obey'd,
Sure no man here will ever dare to break.

[*Enter Jonfon's ghoft, who, by action, removes the fpeaker of the former part of the epilogue.*]

Hold, and give way, for I myfelf will fpeak;
Can you encourage fo much infolence,
And add new faults ftill to the great offence
Your anceftors fo rafhly did commit
Againft the mighty powers of art and wit,
When they condemned thofe noble works of mine,
Sejanus, and my beft love, Catiline.
Repent, or on your guilty heads fhall fall
The curfe of many a rhyming paftoral.
The three bold Beauchamps fhall revive again,
And with the London 'Prentice conquer Spain.
All the dull follies of the former age
Shall find applaufe on this corrupted ftage.

But,

> But, if you pay the great arrears of praise,
> So long since due to my much-injur'd plays,
> From all past crimes I first will set you free,
> And then inspire some one to write like me.

Downs, in a list of plays acted by the king's company at Drury-lane, has placed Every Man in his Humour. I, at first, supposed that it had been revived by the comedians of that house; but Medbourne being taken notice of in the epilogue, as the domestic poet of the playhouse, who was an actor in the duke's company, I am convinced that our stage-historian was in an error, or that this play was revived at both theatres, contrary to an established order of the court, which enjoined the two theatres to divide the old plays between them, and not meddle with one another's property.

Matthew Medbourne, who, in this epilogue, is said to have had no less than ten plays by him, was an excellent actor. He rendered himself acceptable, by his learning and accomplishments, to persons of fashion and taste, and was particularly distinguished by the earl of Dorset, who, not only condescended to mention him in this epilogue, but wrote an epilogue to his translation of Moliere's Tartuffe. Medbourne lived at a time when the state divisions were at the height. He was a Roman Catholic, and warmly attached to the interest of his royal patron the duke of York. Unhappily, perhaps, on account of some imprudent expression, or for some inadvertent behaviour, he was involved in the popish plot, and thrown into Newgate, where he was suffered to perish. Such was the rage of party, that a man of so little consequence as a player was made an object of popular resentment by the

furious

furious politics of Lord Shaftſbury and his colleagues.

I was informed, many years ſince, that Every Man in his Humour was revived at the theatre in Lincoln's-inn-fields about the year 1720: how the parts were diſtributed I could not learn.

Towards the beginning of the year 1750, Mr. Garrick was induced, by his own judgment, or the advice of others, to revive this comedy, and to bring it on his ſtage. He expunged all ſuch paſſages in it as either retarded the progreſs of the plot, or, through length of time, were become obſolute or unintelligible; and theſe were not a few. Of all our old play-wrights, Jonſon was moſt apt to allude to local cuſtoms and temporary follies. Mr. Garrick likewiſe added a ſcene of his own.

Notwithſtanding all the care he had beſtowed in pruning and dreſſing this dramatic tree, he was fearful it would not flouriſh when brought forth to public view. To prevent, therefore, any miſcarriage in the acting of the play, he took an accurate ſurvey of his company, and conſidered their diſtinct and peculiar faculties. He gave to each comedian a part which he thought was in the compaſs of his power to hit off with ſkill. Kitely, the jealous huſband, which requires great art in the performer, he took upon himſelf; to Woodward he aſſigned Bobadil, which has been thought, by many good judges, to have been his maſterpiece in low comedy. Brainworm was played with all the archneſs and varied pleaſantry that could be aſſumed by Yates: Welbred and Young Knowell by Roſs and Palmer. Shuter entered moſt naturally into the follies of a young, ignorant fellow, who thinks

ſmoaking

smoaking tobacco fashionably, and swearing a strange kind of oath, the highest proofs of humour and taste. Winstone, who was tolerated in other parts, in Downright was highly applauded. Old Knowell became the age and person of Berry. Mrs. Ward, a pretty woman, and an actress of considerable talents, acted dame Kitely. Miss Minors, since Mrs. Walker, was the Mrs. Bridget. I must not forget master Matthew, the town gull, which was given, with much propriety, to Harry Vaughan, a brother of Mrs. Pritchard, a man formed by nature for small parts of low humour and busy impertinence; such as Tester in the Suspicious Husband, Simple in the Merry Wives of Windsor, and Simon in the Apprentice.

After all the attention of the acting manager to draw together such a groupe of original actors as were scarce ever collected before, the antiquated phrase of old Ben appeared so strange and was so opposite to the taste of the audience, that he found it no easy matter to make them relish the play. However, by obstinate perseverance, and by retrenching every thing that hurt the ear or displeased the judgment, he brought it at last to be a favourite dramatic dish, which was often presented to full and brilliant audiences.

Not any of the actors, who figured in this comedy, are now living, except Mr. Yates, Mr. Ross and Miss Minors. To what I have said of those who are dead, I shall now only add, that Palmer, who married Miss Prichard, died by an improper draught given him, in his illness, through mistake. Harry Vaughan, by fancying himself co-heir with his sister, Mrs. Pritchard, to large property, which was contested by other claimants,

claimants, (the heirs at law,) exchanged a life of innocence and ease for much disappointment and vexation of mind. He died rich, but neither happy nor respected. However, I believe he thought that he had a right to that of which he had acquired possession.

The frequent rehearsal of this comedy was a convincing proof of Garrick's great anxiety for its public approbation. As no man more perfectly knew the various characters of the drama than himself, his reading a new or revived piece was a matter of instruction, as well as entertainment, to the players. He generally seasoned the dry part of the lecture with acute remarks, shrewd applications to the company present, or some gay jokes, which the comedians of the theatre, who survive their old master, will recollect with pleasure.

As he took infinite pains to inform, he expected an implicit submission to his instructions. A compliance, after all, which could not be expected from men of great professional abilities, such as Yates and Woodward. All that can be expected from genius is, to take the out-line and to observe a few hints towards the colouring of a character; the heightening, or finishing, must be left to the performer.

During the greatest part of the rehearsals of Every Man in his Humour, Woodward seemed very attentive to Garrick's ideas of Bobadil. But, in his absence one morning, he indulged himself in the exhibition of his own intended manner of representation. While the actors were laughing and applauding Woodward, Garrick entered the playhouse, and unperceived, attended to the transaction of the scene. After waiting some time, he
stept

stept on the stage, and cried, " Bravo, Harry ! bravo ! upon my foul, bravo !—Why, now this is—no, no, I can't say this is quite my idea of the thing—Yours is, after all—to be fure, rather —ha !"—Woodward perceiving the manager a little embarraffed, with much feeming modefty, faid, " Sir, I will act the part, if you defire it, exactly according to your notion of it."—" No, no ! by no means, Harry. D—n it, you have actually clenched the matter.—But why, my dear Harry, would not you communicate before ?"

Mrs. Ward was a very favourite actrefs at Edinburgh, when Delane and Sparks exhibited upon the theatre of that city, in the fummer of 1748. Delane, though at that time in the fervice of Mr. Garrick, perhaps inadvertently recommended her to his old mafter, Mr. Rich, who immediately fixed her in his company by articles of agreement. Her firft appearance, at Covent-Garden theatre, was in Cordelia, the winter enfuing, when Quin acted Lear.

Though this actrefs was very attractive in feature and agreeable in figure, yet, it muft be granted, that parts of vigour and loftinefs were much more fuitable to her manner than Cordelia. The high paffions of Hermione were more congenial to her voice and fpirit than a Shore or a Monimia: fhe was a better Califta than a Juliet. She died about twelve years fince. Delane's complaifance to Rich, by being an inftrument of engaging, to that manager, Mrs. Ward, loft him the friendfhip of Garrick, and occafioned a quarrel between them, which ended only with the life of the former. Before this tranfaction, they had been on the moft friendly terms: Garrick had publickly

publickly professed himself the friend of Delane, and took a pleasure in walking with him, in the street, arm in arm. But, '*O world, thy slippery turns!*'* Delane, soon after his arrival from Scotland, accidentally met Garrick in the piazza of Covent-Garden, who not only would not return his salute, but gave him such a look of anger and disdain, as few men, besides himself, had it in their power to bestow. An immediate separation of interest ensued. Delane's articles were given up, and he was hired to Mr. Rich. This actor did not long survive the quarrel. He was a man of spirit, and felt all the disagreeableness of contemptuous treatment. Whether, in consequence of this difference, he applied himself with greater eagerness to his bottle, or whether it was owing to his usual indulgence in the circulation of the glass, it was universally said that he died a martyr to Bacchus. This happened about the year 1750.

Every Man in his Humour, notwithstanding the loss of so many capital performers, who played in it on its revival, continues still to be a play to which the public pays attention. Many of the characters are well adapted to the abilities of the actors, particularly Mr. Smith in Kitely, who, in this part, is not an unworthy successor of our great Roscius; Mr. Palmer in Bobadil, Mr. Dodd in Master Stephen, and Baddeley in Brainworm, are much approved. Their merit appears to greater advantage, as they could not have the same instructions which their predecessors had. Mr. Henderson, when at Drury-lane, tried his skill in Bobadil. Though different in his manner

* Coriolanus.

ner from Woodward, he drew a good portrait of the coward and the bully.—Were he to act it oftner, he would certainly be more warm in his colouring.

The success of Every Man in his Humour encouraged Ben to write Every Man out of his Humour. This he, very judiciously, I think, calls a comic satire. It consists of a variety of characters, exhibiting manners rather in loose and independent scenes than in a regular fable. Downs places this comedy in the list of plays which were revived by the king's company of comedians. But I believe he is guilty of the same mistake which he fell into with respect to Every Man in his humour, which I have sufficiently proved was acted by Betterton's company. Whether Ben Jonson was the first dramatist who introduced upon our stage a grex, who comment upon the action of the several characters in the play, is not very material. He has been followed in this by the Duke of Buckingham and others, and by Mr. Foote lately in some of his farces, in which some of his actors have spoken to others on the stage from the gallery and the boxes, to the no small entertainment of the spectators. This piece has, in my opinion, a great share of comic pleasantry, and, with some judicious alterations, would now afford rational amusement. Some of the characters, it is true, are obsolete through age; others, such as the Envious Man and the Parasite, are of all times and all nations. Macilente and Carlo Buffone will last till doomsday: they are admirably well drawn. The objection of Dr. Hurd, who terms the play a hard delineation of a groupe of simply-existing passions, wholly chimerical, is ill-founded. Some of these parts are

are to be seen now in some shape or other; fashionable shadows of foppery and custom vary with times and circumstances. Who does not see every day a Sogliardo and Fungoso, differently modified, in our metropolis at this instant? In a rude unpolished age, when the people were just emancipated from barbarism by the renovation of literature and the light of reformation, a groupe of new and absurd characters must naturally spring up which would furnish ample materials of ridicule to the comic writers; and who can deny that Jonson has, in this play, laid hold of many growing follies of the times in which he lived?

With submission to so justly-celebrated a writer as Dr. Hurd, I would ask, what is it that constitutes character? Is it not that distinguished passion, or peculiar humour, which separates a man from the rest of his species? Characters are formed from manners, and these are derived from passions. When they are indulged to a certain distinguishing degree, so as to make a man ridiculous or remarkable, we then call him a character. The Muses' Looking-Glass cannot be paralleled with Every Man in his Humour, because in this we have action, which the other wants.

Jonson has, in one part, delineated a character which did not exist perhaps in that full force in his own days, and with such eclat and additional force from certain circumstances, as it has done since. Many striking features of Carlo Buffone will, if I mistake not, be acknowledged to have existed in a late shining comic genius. Let us read Buffone's character given by Cordato:———

' He

' He is one whom the author calls *Carlo Buffone*, an impudent common jester, a violent railer, and an incomprehensible epicure ; one whose company is desired of all men, but beloved of none ; he will sooner lose his soul than a jest, and profane even the most holy thing, to excite laughter ; no honourable or reverend personage whatsoever, that comes within the reach of his eye, but is turned into all manner of variety by his adulterous similies.'

We must grant Jonson the merit of being the first who could fix that uncertain and wandering thing, called *humour*, by a just and accurate definition :

"——When some peculiar quality
Doth so possess a man, that it doth draw
All affects, his spirits, and his powers,
In their constructions, all to run one way,—
This may be truly said to be a *humour*."

This comic satire gave general satisfaction. Queen Elizabeth, drawn by the fame which was spread of it, honoured the play with her presence. Jonson, to pay a respectful compliment to his sovereign, altered the conclusion of his play into an elegant panegyric, spoken by Malicente; which turns upon this simple idea; that her majesty's powerful influence had converted him, the representative of envy, into a contrary character. Mr. Collins, the author of several justly-esteemed poems, first pointed out to me the particular beauties of this occasional address. The reader will not think his time ill-spent in reading the most interesting part of it :

—In

— In the ample and unmeasur'd flood
Of her perfections are my passions drown'd;
And I have now a spirit as sweet and clear
As the most rarified and subtle air.
With which, and with a heart as pure as fire,
Yet humble as the earth, do I implore
Heaven, that she, whose presence hath effected
This change in me, may suffer most late change
In her admir'd and happy government.
May still this island be call'd fortunate!
And rugged treason tremble at the sound,
When fame shall speak it with an emphasis.
Let foreign polity be dull as lead,
And pale invasion come with half a heart,
When he looks upon her blessed soil.
The throat of war be stopp'd within her land,
And turtle-footed Peace dance fairy-rings
About her court; where never may there come
Suspect or danger, but all trust and safety!
Let Flattery be dumb, and Envy blind,
In her dread presence; Death himself admire her;
And may her virtues make him to forget
The use of his inevitable hand!
Fly from her, Age! Sleep, Time, before her throne!
Our strongest walls fall down when she is gone!

Macilente is the abstract of envy in Every Man out of his Humour; *Rancour*, in the *Roman comique* of Scarron, is the same character dilated. This play was acted, by the established comedians, in 1599. Why Jonson left them, and employed the children of the queen's chapel, in preference, to act his Cynthia's revels, is a question that cannot now be easily, if at all, decided.

We have some reason to conjecture, that the acting of Every Man in his Humour must have been attended with certain circumstances unpleasing to the author, or he would not have delivered his next play, ' *As you find it*,' to be acted by children. This comedy, though worth saving from oblivion, does not call, in my opinion, for the eulogium which has been conferred upon it.

In his introduction to his Every Man out of his Humour, the author told the people, with more frankness than discretion, that, if they did not like his play, it must be attributed to their ignorance:

———————If we fail,
We must impute it to this only chance,—
Art hath an enemy call'd ignorance.

In As you find it, he seems to complain of the rude behaviour of an audience, in manifesting their dislike and contempt, by various methods, to a good play; meaning no doubt, one of his own. This charge he renewed. In his dialogue of the boys, at the beginning of Cynthia's Revels, and indeed almost through all his pieces, he seems to be exceedingly sore; for he imprudently provokes the ill-will and contempt of those who must finally condemn or establish his works, and from whom there can be no adequate appeal. Shakspeare modestly courted the good will of his auditors; Jonson defied and affronted them.

His next piece the poetaster, is a satire upon the players, under the pretence of retaliating the abuse he had suffered from Decker. Notwithstanding all he has said to defend himself from the charge of general obloquy on the society of actors, in a dialogue which he tells us was spoken
but

but once, by way of address to the audience, the Poetaster is a formal attack upon the comedians and their profession. Churchill was a generous and fair satirist; Jonson insidiously skulks under the pretence of aiming at one or two of the fraternity, when he really levels his shafts at them all. Some of the players he characterizes under feigned names: such as 'the lean Poluphagus,' by whom I conjecture he means Burbage, who, I have no doubt, acted the lean Macilente. Of him he makes Tucca say,—' He will eat a leg of mutton, while I am in my porridge. His belly is like Barathrum.' By 'Frisker the zany, and good skipping swaggerer,' I have fancied that he meant Kempe, who was celebrated for his ready wit and facetious jesting: however, this is only conjecture. Who he means by 'Mango the fat fool,' is still less in my conception. 'You may bring him,' says Tucca, who is the author's mouth-piece against the comedians; 'but let him not beg rapiers and scarfes in his own familiar playing face, nor roar out his barren bold jests with a tormenting laughter between drunk and dry. Do you hear, Stifftoe? give him warning to forsake his saucy glavering grace and his goggle eye; it does not become him, sirrah!' Lowin was the original Falstaff, and played innumerable parts of humour and pleasantry: perhaps Ben flings this outrageous sarcasm at this actor. We have leave to guess any body, since he spares nobody.

The Poetaster, notwithstanding the author's predilection for it, is one of Jonson's lowest productions: it was conceived in malice and brought forth in anger. It is indeed a contemptible mixture of the serio-comic; where the names of Augustus Cæsar, Mecænas, Virgil, Horace, Ovid, and Tibullus, are all sacrificed upon the altar of private resentment. The translations from the classics are meanly literal, as well as harsh and quaint, and far inferior to those of Chapman, or any other translator of those times. Jonson's Tucca is a wretched copy, or ape, of the inimitable Falstaff. This comical satire, as it is called, closes with an apologetical address to the reader, stuffed with farther abuse upon the players, with a slender exception in favour of *some better natures* amongst them. There is nothing so remarkable in this dialogue as the author's arrogance. After having laboured most strenuously to give proofs of his importance, in a kind of poetic rapture, he thrusts his friends from him, by telling them, ' He will try if Tragedy have a more kind aspect, for her favours he will next pursue.' We must suppose, then, that he was in labour of his great Sejanus.

By the mediation of friends, and most likely by the good-offices of our gentle Shakspeare, a reconciliation was effected between this surly writer and the comedians.

CHAP.

CHAP. XXIV.

Jonson's Sejanus.—Assisted in it by Shakspeare.—Sejanus inferior to Shakspeare's third-rate tragedies.—Jonson's translations from the classics.—His ignorance of decency and decorum.—Defence of Silius commended.—Tiberius and Macro.—Soliloquy of Sejanus.—Catiline.—Condemned originally.—Revived by Charles Hart.—Supposed at the instigation of Buckingham, Dorset, &c.—Cicero's speeches immoderately long.—Cicero's character rejected, by Major Mohun, for Cethegus.—His excellence in the part.—Jonson's ladies.—Leonard Digges.—His verses on Jonson's three comedies.—Jonson's frown.—Acquainted with the Duke of Buckingham when the duke was a boy.—Stage-learning required for Jonson's characters.

SHAKSPEARE not only acted a part in Sejanus, but wrote some scenes for it, as originally represented. Of this Jonson takes notice in an advertisement to an edition of this play printed in 1605; and, though he does not mention his coadjutor's name, he points him out by the appellation of a happy genius. However, it is remarkable, though he condescended to be the avowed fellow-labourer of Chapman, Marston, Rowley, and others, he assures the reader, with a sneer, that he would not join his own inferior matter to that of the great poet; but he wrote over again those scenes which had been wrought into the piece by the pen of Shakspeare. Who does not wish that Shakspeare had put as high a value upon his true brilliants as Ben did upon his jewels of paste? The scenes, rejected by Jonson, Shakspeare did not preserve. I have had some little suspicion, that Shakspeare's part of this tragic entertainment might possibly be that alone which escaped public censure; the play, he tells us himself, was universally exploded. Nay, he says that the play did not fare better from the spectators, than the body of Sejanus did from the Roman mob.

Ben, notwithstanding, greatly valued himself upon this tragedy. Let any candid judge examine it with the second or third rate tragedies of Shakspeare, and he will find it far inferior to the spirit that reigns in the worst of them.

If, in his historical pieces, our admirable bard is sometimes blameable for overloading his scenes with multiplicity of business, and with incidents undramatic, Ben Jonson, in the selection of historical events, is far less happy than his rival. The speeches of his principal characters are long and tedious, and neither interesting from sentiment, passion, or business. His translations from the classics are tiresome and disgusting, and retard, rather than forward, the progress of the play. When the tragedy is brought, by the death of Sejanus, to its proper period, (and which is pompously and too circumstantially related from Juvenal,) the curtain is not suffered to fall till you are tortured with, what might have been well spared, an odious relation of the cruel deaths of his young son, and his daughter, a child who is first vitiated by the common executioner, to be made a legal victim of justice to the state. This man, the frequenter of courts, the scholar of Camden, the friend of Selden, and the companion

nion of Sir Harry Savile, had no knowledge of decorum and decency.

But, that I may not be thought to view this author's writings with a partial malignity, let me candidly confess there is something noble and affecting in the defence of Silius, whose voluntary death in the senate is striking and truly dramatic; that Tiberius's dissembled knowledge of Sejanus's designs, with his employing Macro to check the pride and insolence of his minion, are masterly touched; and the fine soliloquy of Sejanus, in which he enumerates the slaughter of his enemies, cannot be too much applauded.

To have done at once with Jonson's tragic poetry, let us now proceed to his Catiline, which Lord Dorset calls ' his best love, Catiline.'

We have the author's testimony that this play was condemned in the acting. It cannot now be known whether it was afterwards revived before the playhouses were shut up in the beginning of the civil wars. I rather incline to think it must have been, by some means, brought again on the stage before the Restoration; some time after which it was revived by Charles Hart.—This great actor, having a considerable venture in the theatre, would not, without some prospect of success, have run the risk of decorating a piece in which such a number of characters were included.

The Duke of Buckingham and Lord Dorset were admirers of Jonson to a degree of idolatry; it is very probable, that, by liberal promises, they encouraged the actors to bring forward this forgotten tragedy. Certain it is, that the play was acted several times during the reign of Charles II. The action of Hart, in Catiline, was universally

universally applauded; and this contributed to keep alive what otherwise would have soon been lost to the public.—' Hart's action,' said the great critic, Rymer, ' could throw a lustre on the most wretched characters; and he so far dazzled the eyes of the spectator by it, that the deformities of the poet could not be discerned.' Jonson has, besides, placed Catiline in such situations, and given sentiments so correspondent to his ambitious and savage mind, that a good actor could not fail to improve them to the delight of an intelligent audience. But, when we allow all this, and more, Catiline upon the whole, is a very languid and tedious entertainment. Nothing but a very strong prepossession in the author's favour could have induced an audience to hear with patience the speeches of Cicero, which, bating the interruptions of a line or two, are extended to the immeasurable length of one hundred and seventy lines. A great deal of Sallust, and almost the whole of Cicero's Catilinarian orations, are translated verbally. This in Jonson's age, was more unnecessary, perhaps, than in our own: the classics were in every body's hands. The last editors of Shakspeare have, with singular diligence, given a list of all the translations from the Greek, and Roman authors published in the reigns of Elizabeth and James; and it is almost astonishing to think what floods of science and learning were poured in from these classic fountains.

The part of Cicero must have been an intolerable burden to an actor of Stentorian lungs, unless the orations were considerably curtailed. Major Mohun, who is celebrated by my Lord Rochester for the wonder of actors, rejected Cicero,

cero, and took a much shorter part, that of Cethegus, his acting of which the same nobleman much applauds. The manners of this play are, in one place particularly, more censurable than those of Sejanus. In the grand meeting of the conspirators, one of them, by action, tempts a young lad to submit to his infamous passion; upon his unwillingness to comply, Catiline threatens him with instant death if he persists to refuse gratifying the other's more than brutal inclination. This, I suppose, Ben would call the truth of history and highly characteristical. But surely he must have read and translated Horace's Art of Poetry with little taste who could be guilty of such indecency. Jonson's women are, in general, disagreeable company; they are vicious and vulgar, and make the author smell too much of low company and the brothel. We have, indeed, one modest Celia, and my good Dame Kitely, to counterbalance his large number of rampant ladies. The scene, in Catiline, between Curius and Fulvia, by the conduct of which the conspiracy is brought to light, is naturally imagined and dramatically conducted.—— Jonson, by his knowledge of Roman manners, customs, attires, &c. avoids tolerably well the common fault of our old dramatists, who are sure to travel with the manners of our metropolis to all parts of the globe.

The critics who lived in the same age with the author, and all who have succeeded till within these twenty or thirty years, have bestowed the most superlative commendations upon Volpone, the Silent Woman, and the Alchemist; and yet we find, by a contemporary, who seems to have no mean opinion of these comedies, that they were exhibited

exhibited to empty benches, at a time when the name of Shakspeare was a charm sufficient to draw multitudes to see his dramatic works. Mr. Malone has quoted, in his supplement to Shakspeare, a copy of verses, by Leonard Digges, prefixed to Shakspeare's poems, where we have the following account of Jonson's great chef-d'œuvres:

> And tho' the Fox and subtle Alchemist,
> Long intermitted, could not quite be miss'd;
> Tho' these have sham'd the ancients, and might raise
> Their author's merit with a crown of bays;
> Yet these, sometimes, ev'n at a friend's desire,
> Acted, have scarce defray'd the sea-coal fire
> And door-keepers:—when, let Falstaff come,
> Hal, Poins, the rest,—you scarce shall have a room,
> All is so pester'd. Let but Beatrice
> And Benedick be seen! lo! in a trice,
> The cock-pit, gall'ries, boxes, all, are full, &c.

In another place of the same poem:

> When, some new day, they would not brook a line
> Of tedious, tho' well-labour'd, Catiline;
> Sejanus, too, was irksome——

And this seems to be a fair and just account of the regard in which Jonson was generally held. He was never supported by the public voice, though kept alive by the critics and the excellent performance of the actors. He had bullied the authors of his own times into an extraordinary opinion of his vast merit; and, when he died, he left such a frown behind him, that he frightened all succeeding dramatic poets and critics, who were afraid to censure, what, in their hearts, they neither admired nor approved. I have already

ready given my opinion that some of our leading nobility, and other court critics, made it their business to stimulate the players to revive their favourite author, though I am persuaded, the greatest part of the audiences had no appetite for him. The Duke of Buckingham has found room in his Rehearsal to give praise to Ben Jonson, though he no where mentions Shakspeare. But the duke, it seems, conversed with Ben when his grace was a boy of about thirteen, and the poet was near his grand climacterique, and thence conceived such a veneration for him, that it never left him afterwards.

It was a constant complaint of the old actors, who lived in Queen Anne's time, that if Jonson's plays were intermitted for a few years, they could not know how to personate his characters, they were so difficult, and their manners so distant, from those of all other authors. To preserve them required a kind of stage learning, which was traditionally hoarded up. Mosca, in Volpone, when he endeavours to work upon the avarice of Corvino, and to induce him to offer his wife to the pretendedly sick voluptuary, pronounces the word *think*, seven or eight times: there is a difficulty arises here in various pause and difference of sound. Many niceties of this kind were observed by the old comedians, which are now absolutely lost to the stage.

CHAP. XXV.

Fable of Volpone.—Lucian's Dialogues.—Praise of The Fox.—The laſt act condemned.—The actors in Volpone.—Booth, Wilks, Cibber, Mills, Jonſon.—Mrs. Clive.—Mr. Boman, &c.—Garrick's intention to revive Volpone.—The Silent Woman.—Revival in 1752.—*Character of Moroſe.—Difficulty in acting Ben Jonſon's characters.—His plays obſolete.—A ſweet ſonnet.—Cartwright and Mohun.—Reſpect paid by Booth, Wilks, and Cibber, to Jonſon's Silent Woman.—Ben Jonſon the actor.—Shepherd.—The Alchemiſt.—Bad cataſtrophe.—Abel Drugger.—The. Cibber.—Garrick and Weſton.—Yates.—The two Palmers.—Ben Griffin and Ben Jonſon.—Sir Epicure Mammon.—Harper and Love.—Doll Common.—Mrs. Clive and Mrs. Pritchard.*

THE Fable of Volpone is choſen with judgment, and is founded upon avarice and luxury. The paying obſequious and conſtant courtſhip to childleſs rich people, with a view to obtain from them bountiful legacies in return, has been a practice of all times, and in all nations. There is in Lucian, the father of true ridicule, an admirable dialogue, on this ſubject, between Pluto and Mercury. An old man of ninety is aſſiduouſly courted by ſeveral young fellows, who, in hopes of being his heirs, perform the loweſt and meaneſt offices to him. Pluto orders Mercury to carry off theſe raſcals, who are dividing, in their minds, the old fellow's riches, to the infernal ſhades; but commands him to double, nay, treble, the age of him who is the object of their obſequiouſneſs.

sequiousness. Lucian has no less than five or six dialogues on the same subject.

In the comedy of The Fox, there is not much to be censured, except the language, which is so pedantic and stuck so full of Latinity, that few, except the learned, can perfectly understand it. 'Jonson, says Dr. Young, brought all the ancients upon his head: by studying to speak like a Roman, he forgot the language of his country.'

The conduct of the plot in the first four acts, except the mountebank scene, is truly admirable. The last act is, in my opinion, quite farcical. That a man of Volpone's sagacity should venture to appear in public, in the disguise of a mountebank, to be an eye witness of a lady's beauty, of which he had heard only from report, and after escaping from the apprehended consequences of this exorbitant frolic, which had brought him within the censure of a court of judicature, upon the bare declaration of the judges in his favour, and against those he had caused to be unjustly accused; that he should again assume another shape, that of an apparitor or tipstaff; make a pretended will; leave all his money, jewels, and effects, pretendedly to so wretched a fellow as a pimp and parasite; and all this with no other view than to mortify, insult, and abuse, those whom he had gulled, while yet the sentence of the court was depending, is a matter as absurd and improbable as any thing acted at the Italian comedy.

In the year 1731, the elder Mills acted Volpone; Wilks, Mosca; Colley Cibber, Corvino; Ben Jonson, Corbaccio; Mrs. Horton, Lady Would-be; and Celia by Mrs. Butler. About three

three years after, it was acted to still more advantage, for Quin excelled Mills in Volpone. In the Mountebank he assumed all the art, trick, and voluble impudence, of a charlatan; though W. Mills, who succeeded Wilks in Mosca, fell below his predecessor, yet his father, who submitted to play Corvino, was superior to C. Cibber in that part. Cibber seemed, I thought, to jest with the character. Mills was in earnest, and had a stronger voice to express passionate and jealous rage than the other. Jonson kept his old part, but Milward's Voltore was a fine copy of law oratory. Mrs. Clive, I need not say, gave infinite entertainment in Lady Wou'd-be. Though Celia is but a short part, to Mrs. Butler's great commendation, she rendered it extremely interesting.

To omit mentioning the part of the first avocatori, or superior judge, would be an act of injustice; for it was represented with great propriety by the venerable Mr. Boman, at that time verging to the eightieth year of his age. This actor was the last of the Bettertonian school. By the remains of this man, the spectators might guess at the perfection to which the old masters in acting had arrived. Boman pronounced the sentence upon the several delinquents, in the comedy, with becoming gravity, grace, and dignity.

Mr. Garrick had long wished to revive Volpone, and to act the principal character. The parts were transcribed and delivered to the actors, but the acting of the play was superseded by some means not known.

The writers, upon dramatic poetry, of the last century, and during a considerable part of the present,

present, have concurred in extolling the merits of the Silent Woman. Lowin, I think, originally acted Morose, and Taylor, True-Wit. Mr. Dryden, in his Essay on Dramatic Poetry, has given a very advantageous character of this play. After all the panegyric bestowed upon it, the play is of that number which needs much forgiveness, if it really has a title to much commendation. The great licentiousness of its dialogue was no obstacle to its success when originally performed; nor, in the reign of Charles II. when revived. But, as the age advanced in decency of manners, the less could the Silent Woman be tolerated. When it was revived, about thirty years since, under the management of Mr. Garrick, with perseverance it was dragged on for a few nights. The managers acquired neither profit nor reputation by the exhibition of it. Some expressions met with severe marks of the spectators displeasure. The character of Morose, upon whose peevish and perverse humour the plot of the comedy depends, is that of a whimsical recluse, whose disposition can bear no sound but that which he utters himself. If this were the whole of his character, he would still be a good object for comic satire, but the melancholy of Morose degenerates into malice and cruelty. In extreme old age, to disinherit a worthy young man, his nephew, he enters into the bonds of matrimony. The schemes therefore which are contrived to disturb his repose and torment his mind, are proper medicines for such a man, and justified by the strictest morality.

But, besides the licentiousness of the manners, and quaintness of expression, in the Silent Woman, the frequent allusions to forgotten customs

and

and characters render it impossible to be ever revived with any probability of success. To understand Jonson's comedies perfectly, we should have before us a satirical history of the age in which he lived. I question whether the diligence of Mr. Steevens and Mr. Malone could dig up a very complete explanation of this author's allusions. Mr. Colman, after all the pains and skill he could bestow on this comedy, found that it was labour lost; there was no reviving the dead. The audience were as much disgusted with Jonson's old ruffs and bands, as the wits of James I. were with Hyeronimo's old cloak and the Spanish tragedy.

It must yet be confessed, that the gentlemen of this comedy, though perhaps too learned for the present day, converse with an easy gaiety and liberal familiarity, superior to any of this writer's productions. In the first act there is a sonnet, which, for the vivacity and elegance of its turn of thought, I cannot forbear transcribing:

> Still to be neat, still to be dress'd
> As you were going to a feast;
> Still to be powder'd, still perfum'd;
> Lady, 'tis to be presum'd,
> Though art's hid causes are not found,
> All is not sweet, all is not sound.
> Give me a look, give me a face,
> That makes simplicity a grace;
> Robes loosely flowing, hair as free;
> Such sweet neglect more taketh me
> Than all th' adulteries of art,
> That strike my eyes, but not my heart.

The

The author, agreeably to his old custom, has made very free with the ancients: he has borrowed from Juvenal, Ovid de Arte Amandi, and Plautus's Aulularia. —

We are told, that the Fox was conceived and brought forth in six weeks. But Jonson's dramatic muse lay fallow for four years; for Volpone was acted in 1605, and the Silent Woman not till the year 1609. Some new quarrel with the established comedians, I suppose, caused him to have recourse again to his children of the Revels, though he had lost his favourite boy, Sal. Pavy, whose histrionical abilities, and wonderful skill in representing old men, though not arrived to his fourteenth year, he celebrated in a copy of verses to his memory.

Such was the authority of Jonson's name, that the king's comedians, established at the Restoration, claiming a prior right of choice to the Duke of York's players, seized upon Ben Jonson's three most esteemed comedies and his two tragedies.

Cartwright, who was a bookseller as well as an actor, played Morose. He is mentioned by name in the Rehearsal.———Major Mohun was celebrated for True-Wit. The famous Lacy acted Captain Otter.

About fifty or sixty years since, great respect was paid to this comedy; for Booth, Wilks, the elder Mills, and Colley Cibber, acted the Dauphin, True-Wit, Clerimont, and Sir John Daw. Such an exhibition of comic distress, in old Ben Jonson's Morose, I have hardly ever seen in any other actor. He and Weston are the only comedians I can remember, that, in all the parts they represented, absolutely forgot themselves.

I have

I have seen very great players, nay, superior, in some respects, to them, at least in the art of colouring and high finishing, when on the stage laugh at a blunder of a performer or some accidental impropriety of the scene: but these men were so truly absorbed in character, that they never lost sight of it. Jonson stayed on the stage to the last, till within about two years of eighty; but his very dregs were respectable. He died in 1742; and, a few months before his death, was out of humour, that the agent of the Dublin theatre, who came over on purpose to engage Mr. Garrick for the summer-months, had not made overtures to him. Otter was well acted by Shepherd, and Sir Amorous La Foole with vivacity by Theophilus Cibber.

The Alchemist was Ben Jonson's last comedy of merit, for afterwards he produced nothing very estimable. This play is, I think, equal to any of this author's, in plot, character, and comic satire. The catastrophe is surely a bad one; a gentleman of fortune joining with his knavish servant, to cheat a parcel of bubbles of their money and goods, is equally mean and immoral. This play kept possession of the stage long after the imposture it was written to detect had ceased. It is worked up with amazing art; and, as its foundation is laid in avarice and imposition, it affords a groupe of comic characters and variety of stage-business. However, it must be owned, that, for these last forty years, it has been supported by the action of a favourite Abel Drugger. Mr. Garrick freed the stage from the false spirit, ridiculous squinting, and vile grimace, which, in Theophilus Cibber, had captivated the public for several years, by introducing a more
natural

natural manner of difplaying the abfurdities of a foolifh tobacconift. At the fame time, juftice calls upon us to allow, that the fimplicity of Wefton almoft exceeded the fine art of a Garrick, whofe numberlefs excellences may fpare a tribute of praife to this genuine child of nature. I cannot omit, in this place, to obferve, that Mr. Garrick, by his own authority, intrenched upon the part of Kaftril, acted incomparably by Mr. Yates, in the 4th act of the play; for the challenging of Surly, and driving him off the ftage, belongs properly to the angry boy, and not to Abel, who, inftead of being an auxiliary, took the field to himfelf. Colley Cibber I have feen act Subtle with great art; the elder Mills at the fame time played Face with much fhrewd fpirit and ready impudence. The two Palmers have fucceffively acted Face with much archnefs and folid characteriftic bronze. Ben Griffin and Ben Jonfon were much admired for their juft reprefentation of the canting puritanical preacher and his folemn deacon the botcher; there was an affected foftnefs in the former which was finely contrafted by the fanatical fury of the other.—— Griffin's features feemed ready to be relaxed into a fmile, while the ftiff mufcles and fierce eye of the other admitted of no fupplenefs or compliance. There is ftill to be feen a fine print of them in thefe characters, from a painting of Vanbleek: they are very ftriking refemblances of both comedians.

It has been faid, that Sir Epicure Mammon was drawn to imitate or outdo Falftaff. I confefs I fee very little, if any, refemblance. Sir Epicure is a fine portrait of a man learned in the

art

art of luxury, gulled by his extreme rapacity and high relish for extravagant pleasure.

I have never seen an adequate representer of Sir Epicure, from Harper down to Love. The first seemed to have been taught by one who had juster conceptions of what was to be done in the part than the player could execute. The outline was well drawn by Love; but there was a deficiency of glowing and warm tints which such a rich dupe in folly required, and the character amply afforded. Love's conceptions of the part were just, but his want of power to execute his meaning rendered his acting imperfect. The original actor of Sir Epicure, Lowin, was said to have represented it in a most perfect style of playing. Doll Common fell into Mrs. Clive's hands about fifty years ago. How she came afterwards into the possession of Mrs. Pritchard, while her friend was still in the company, I know not. If I remember rightly, the former, by lessening the vulgarity of the prostitute, did not give so just an idea of her as the latter. Mrs. Pritchard, by giving a full scope to her fancy as well as judgment, produced a complete resemblance of the practised and coarse harlot in Madam Doll. *

---

* Dr. Johnson was the first who ventured to attack Jonson's infallibility in the following excellent lines:

> Then Jonson came, instructed from the school,
> To please in method and invent by rule.
> His studious patience and laborious art,
> By regular approach, assail'd the heart.
> Cold approbation gave the lingering bayes,
> For those who durst not censure, scarce could praise,
> A mortal born, he met the general doom,
> But left, like Egypt's kings, a lasting tomb.
>
> Macbeth.

Macbeth.

CHAP. XXVI.

Conjectures on the author's design in writing the tragedy of Macbeth.—Dr. Johnson's observations on witchcraft.——Shakspeare's use of vulgar errors.—Davenant's alteration of Macbeth.— Taste for rhyming plays in the reign of Charles II. —Betterton obliged to submit to his superiors.— Defence of the modern stage-witches.—Waxen image of K. Duffus.—A curious poisoning girdle. —King James I. and Sir John Harrington.— Buchanan's dream.—Studied in death and Safe towards your love and honour explained.— Sickness, Thomson.—Crown of Scotland not hereditary.—Reason for Macbeth's treason.—Pity in the figure of a new-born child.—Lady Macbeth and Clytemnestra.—Philip of Macedon compared to a sponge.—Burbage.—Betterton.—Mills unequal to Macbeth.—Anecdote of a country gentleman.—Quin.—Mossop.—Garrick.—Cashel.— Anecdote of him and an insidious rival.—Both died about the same time.

THE author had more than one thing in view when he wrote the tragedy of Macbeth. James I. loved the muses, and, to his own and the poet's honour, distinguished our Shakspeare by particular marks of favour. His plays, we have the authority of Ben Jonson to aver, gave the king great delight; and our best editors speak of a letter which James wrote to him in his own hand: a very singular mark of royal favour, and an evident proof of the king's good taste, humanity and condescension.

To compliment his royal master as the descendant of Banquo, and the first of our monarchs,

'That twofold balls and treble sceptres carry'd,'

was one main motive to the choice of the subject. James's belief in witchcraft, and his pretended knowledge of dæmonology, on which subject he published a volume, was, I believe, another inducement in order to gain his prince's favour. In an account Sir James Harrington has given of a long conference he had with James, he informs us that a considerable part of the king's discourse turned upon witchcraft. I farther believe that there was another, and a political, reason which prevailed upon Shakspeare to make a part of the Scottish history the subject of a play. The English and Scotch, united under one king, was a splendid novelty, as well as a matter of great consequence to both. The perpetual wars, which had been carried on with great animosity, for above five or six hundred years, between the inhabitants of the northern and southern parts of the island, had contributed to embitter the spirits of both, and the sudden establishment of government under one prince could not immediately remove that displeasure which had so long irritated them. Shakspeare, therefore, chose a subject which he thought would render the Scots important in their own eyes, and in the opinion of their new allies and fellow subjects. He has, besides, very happily contrived to celebrate

lebrate the humanity, courage, and generosity, of his own countrymen, in the same piece. The lawful heir to the crown of Scotland is honourably maintained and supported, in the court of an English king, by the bravery of whose subjects the banished prince is restored, and the usurper defeated. This was a fair and honourable method of making court to both English and Scotch.

Dr. Johnson's observations on witchcraft are learned and instructive: nothing can be added to them, at least by me.

The impressions made on the mind of Shakspeare, respecting witches, fairies, and inchantment, produced, in his riper years, such amazing descriptions of the supposed powers, manners, and magic charms, of these imaginary beings, as were wonderfully suited to the credulous age in which he lived. Like other great poets, he took advantage of the popular superstition to create such phantoms of the imagination, which the weak and credulous believed as implicitly as the articles of their creed, while the more sagacious considered them as efforts of fancy and effusions of genius, which contributed to the main design of the poet,—to delight.

At the Restoration, few of our author's plays were written to the palate of the court and those who assumed the direction of the public amusements. After Macbeth had been thrown aside, or neglected for some years, Sir William Davenant undertook to refine and reduce it, as near as possible, to the standard of the taste in vogue. He likewise brought it, as well as he could, to the resemblance of an opera. In the musical part he was assisted by Mr. Locke, an eminent master of music.

music. It must be confessed the songs of Hecate, and the other witches, have a solemn adaption to the beings for whom they were composed. Dances of furies were invented for the incantation-scene in the fourth act, and near fifty years since I saw our best dancers employed in the exhibition of infernal spirits. Had Davenant stopped here, it had been well for his reputation, but this ill-instructed admirer of Shakspeare altered the plan of the author's design, and destroyed that peculiarity which distinguishes Macbeth from several of our author's pieces. The jingle of rhyme delighted the ears of our court critics, for no other reason, which I can discover, but because the plays of the French nation, and especially their tragedies, wore the chiming fetters; but the dramatic poets of France knew that their language was too weak for blank verse, or for lines of twelve feet, without the assistance of rhyme, and therefore, what was mere necessity in them, the false judges of our language considered as an essential beauty.

In the Memoirs of Mr. Garrick, I have quoted some part of a scene between Macbeth and his lady, upon the most serious and important subject, where poverty of sentiment is only exceeded by wretchedness of rhyme. Davenant had, indeed, disfigured the whole piece, yet, notwithstanding all his added deformities and sad mutilations, so much of the original Macbeth was still retained, that it continued, from the revival in 1665 to 1744, a very favourite entertainment of the stage. Betterton, who was then at the head of the duke of York's company, under Sir William Davenant, whatever his own taste might be, was obliged

to

to fall in with the views of his master and the fashion of the times.

Happily for the lovers of Shakspeare, Mr. Garrick, some years before he was a patentee, broke through the fetters of foolish custom and arbitrary imposition: he restored Macbeth to the public almost in the same dress it was left us in, by the author. A scene or two, which were not conducive to the action, he threw out in representation; others that were too long he judiciously pruned; very few additions were made, except in some passages of the play necessary to the better explanation of the writer's intention. He composed, indeed, a pretty long speech for Macbeth, when dying, which, though suitable perhaps to the character, was unlike Shakspeare's manner, who was not prodigal of bestowing, abundance of mater on characters in that situation. But Garrick excelled in the expression of convulsive throes and dying agonies, and would not lose any opportunity that offered to shew his skill in that part of his profession.

Act I. Scene I.

FIRST WITCH.

When shall we three meet again?

It has been an old complaint of stage critics, that the parts of the witches are always distributed amongst the low comedians, who, by mistaking the sense of the author, render those sentiments ridiculous which were designed by him to be spoken with gravity and solemnity. Should we suppose this charge to be well founded, it would not be a very easy task to remove it; for the

tragedians

tragedians are all employed in various parts of the drama, suited to their several abilities, so that none but the comic actors are left to wear gowns, beards, and coifs. But, I confess, I do not see the propriety of the accusation. There is, in the witches, something odd and peculiar, and approaching to what we call humour. The manners bestowed on these beings are more suitable to our notions of comic than tragic action, and better fitted to Yates and Edwin than Henderson and Smith. Nor do I see any impropriety in the manner adopted by the present comedians, who have too much understanding to sacrifice sentiment to grimace, or propriety to buffoonery. From the dramatis personæ of Davenant's Macbeth, we see the parts of the witches given to the low comedians of those times, and in this the alterer, who had seen plays at the Globe, and in Blackfriers, long before the civil wars, followed, in all probability, the practice of the old stage.

WITCH.

Weary sev'nnights nine times nine
Shall he dwindle, peak, and pine.

The Highlands of Scotland seem to have been the favourite resort of witches and inchanters, where they are supposed to have performed their most powerful charms and diabolical incantations; and more particularly the town of Foris, near which place Macbeth was first accosted by these beings. A waxen image of King Duffus, says Buchanan, was found roasting at a fire, in that town, before some infernal hags, who were immediately seized and punished; upon the destroying the image, the king, it is said, recovered. Buchanan did not rely much on the truth of the
story,

story, but gave it as it was related by former writers, though he could not find it authenticated by ancient record. This strange power, of weakening or killing the bodies of men at a distance, is of very ancient date. Lambard, in his Topographical Dictionary, mentions a curious girdle, which was so strongly poisoned as to kill a man at a considerable distance; it was intended, by a certain person or persons to dispatch the Dean of York. The girdle was brought to Smithfield, as heretical, and there burnt.

WITCHES.

The weird sisters hand in hand.

To the learned notes of Dr. Warburton and Mr. Steevens, upon the word *weird*, I shall only add, that the glossarist of Douglas's translation of Virgil derives *weird* from the Anglo-Saxon *wyrd*, fatum, fortuna, eventus; *Wwyrde*, Fata, Parcæ. The old Scotch curse, of ' waeworth him,' is apparently derived from *weird*, or *weyward*. These weyward sisters seem to be akin to the Eumenides of the Greeks. The Furies are prototypes of the northern Parcæ.

BANQUO.

——————*What are these,*
So wither'd, and so wild in their attire?

When James I. asked Sir John Harrington, ' Why the devil did work more with ancient women than others?' Sir John replied, ' We were taught hereof in Scripture, *where it is told, that the devil walketh in dry places.*'

WITCH.

All hail, Macbeth! hail to thee, thane of Glamis!

In the relation of this part of the hiftory, Buchanan differs entirely from Hollingfhead, who copied the tranflator of Boetius. He relates, that, when he was at a diftance from the court, Macbeth, on a certain night, dreamt that he faw three women, of an auguft and more-than human form, who faluted him by the feveral titles of Angus and Murray, and, laftly, of King.

MACBETH.

*————My dull brain was wrought
With things forgot.*

'I was ruminating on matters not worth your hearing or my remembrance.'

Scene IV.

MALCOLM.

As one that had been ftudy'd in his death.

'Studied in his death' is a phrafe borrowed from the theatre: to be ftudied in a part is to have got it by rote, or to have made yourfelf mafter of it. Mr. Steevens hath, with great probability, fuppofed, that, in the defcription of Cawdor's death, the author had a retrofpect to the behaviour of Effex at his execution. He was, by James himfelf, efteemed to be one of his martyrs; and it is not improbable that Shakfpeare was perfonally acquainted with the dear and unfortunate friend of his patron Southampton.

MACBETH.

MACBETH.

> Which do but what they should, by doing every thing
> Safe towards your love and honour.

The several proposed emendations of this passage, by Mr. Theobald, Dr. Warburton, Dr. Johnson, and Dr. Kenrick, are by no means satisfactory. Dr. Johnson candidly doubts his alteration of *safe* to *shapes*; the *fiefs*, or *fief'd*, of Dr. Warburton, is not admissible; and Kenrick's *ward*, though the most plausible, does not, I believe, come up to the intention of the author. I have before me a copy of Shakspeare in folio, the second edition, which formerly belonged to Mr. William Thomson, of Queen's College, Oxford, author of a poem on Sickness: in the margin he puts a question, whether it should not be *life* and *honour* instead of *love* and *honour?* and this conjecture is submitted to the reader, as at least preferable to any emendation as yet advanced.

MACBETH.

> The Prince of Cumberland!—that is a step
> On which I must fall down, or else o'er-leap.

The mind of Macbeth had been greatly agitated by the preceding prophecies of the witches, and the completion of part of them. His fancy had presented to his mind the accomplishment of the whole, by an act, the thought of which alone had struck him with reluctant horror. He seems to have resembled Hazael, in the Scriptures, who, being told, by the prophet Elisha, he should bring terrible calamities upon the people of Israel, cried out, ' Is thy servant a dog, that he should do these things?' But the poet artfully throws in fresh fuel to stimulate his ambition, by the King's nominating his son Prince of Cumberland. The crown of Scotland was not, as Mr. Steevens has observed, hereditary; and every reader of Scottish history will be convinced, that prudence and necessity both co-operated to prevent a regular succession of the son to the father in that kingdom. The kings of Scotland were so often immaturely destroyed, by foreign wars, factions nobility, or private treachery, that it was wisely ordered the crown should devolve on the next of kin arrived to maturity of age and ripeness of understanding, and not to the son of the deceased monarch under age. This was the practice in that kingdom for many ages. Duncan, by appointing his son, then a minor,* Prince of Cumberland, a dignity like that of Prince of Wales with us, cut off all Macbeth's hopes of gaining the crown in case the King should have died before Malcolm arrived to years of maturity. Buchanan says expressly, that, by this action, Duncan had given him sufficient cause of discontent.

Scene VII.

MACBETH.

——————— But, in these cases,
We still have judgment here, that we but teach
Bloody instructions.

The best comment on this passage is to be read in the preface to Sir Walter Raleigh's History of the World, and more particularly in the following quotation

* Vixdum puberem. Buchan. Hist. lib. 7.

quotation from it: 'For those kings, which have sold the blood of others at a low rate, have but made a market for their own enemies to buy of theirs at the same price.'

MACBETH.

————————Besides, this Duncan
Hath borne his faculties so meek, hath been
So clear in his great office——————

The only fault, attributed by historians to the unhappy Duncan, was excess of humanity and gentleness of disposition.—'Vir summa humani-
'tate,' says Buchanan, 'ac majore erga suos
'indulgentia quam in rege par erat.'

IDEM.

And Pity, like a naked new-born babe
Striding the blast, or heaven's cherubin hors'd
Upon the sightless couriers of the air,
Shall blow the horrid deed in ev'ry eye,
That tears shall drown the wind.

The author, not satisfied with presenting us with that tender and beautiful image of pity, a new-born babe, rises to the more sublime idea of an angel mounted on the wings of the wind, to communicate the disastrous news of a monarch's murder to the world. The thought seems to have been borrowed from the eighteenth psalm: 'He rode upon the cherubim and did fly; he came flying upon the wings of the wind!'

Fenton, in his tragedy of Mariamne, in the following lines of Sohemus to Salome, makes Pity young and short-lived:

——————— In diſtant ages paſt,
Pity dy'd young, of grief, they ſay, to ſee
An eagle wreak his malice on a wren.

LADY MACBETH.

——————————Was the hope drunk
Wherein you dreſs'd yourſelf?

In other words, 'Were you ſober when you firſt entertained the conception of killing the king?'

The undaunted ſpirit and determinedly-wicked reſolution of Macbeth's wife are no where to be matched, in any female character of the ancient Greek drama, except in the Clytemneſtra of Æſchylus. Their ſituations are different, but their characters bear a great reſemblance. Both are haughty and intrepid, artful and cruel, in the extreme: Clytemneſtra plans the murder of Agamemnon, her huſband, and is herſelf the aſſaſſin; Lady Macbeth not only encourages her huſband to kill the King, but enjoys the fact when it is done; the remorſe of the murderer ſhe conſiders as puſillanimity, and helps to remove the appearance of guilt from him by ſmearing the faces of the ſleeping grooms

LADY MACBETH.

——————————What not put upon
His *ſpongy* officers?

Men drenched in liquor are with great propriety compared to *ſponges*. When Æſchines praiſed Philip King of Macedon for his abilities in drinking, Demoſthenes told him, 'that was a commendation fit for a *ſponge*.'

Of the original actors in Macbeth we can form no judgment; for nothing is to be found relating to them in books, nor has tradition handed down any thing concerning them. We may indeed conjecture, that Burbage, who exhibited Richard III. was, by the author, selected to represent Macbeth. Not only because he was the first tragedian of the times, but, from his performing characters of a similar cast, we may suppose him to have been better adapted to it than Taylor, (another eminent actor in tragedy,) or any player of that age.

The Tatler has celebrated Betterton for his excellence in Macbeth as well as other principal tragic parts. Cibber has not particularly distinguished this great comedian for his performance of this character; that he acted it to the very verge of his life, I learned in a conversation with Mr. Ryan. Though Booth was one of the company of comedians who obtained a licence in the year 1711, soon after the death of Betterton, Wilks, with great partiality, gave Macbeth to Mr. John Mills, a player whom he patronised. But Mills was deficient in genius to display the various passions and turbulent scenes of the character. Mills was, in person, inclined to the athletic size; his features large, though not expressive; his voice was manly and powerful, but not flexible; his action and deportment decent. In voice and person he was not very unlike Mr. Edward Berry, whom Colley Cibber used to term a second old Mills. I have seen him in Macbeth; but neither his manner of speaking, his action, nor his deportment, made any impression on my mind greatly to his advantage. He spoke, indeed,

indeed, the celebrated foliloquy on the progrefs of time, beginning with 'To-morrow! to-morrow! and to-morrow!' with propriety and feeling, and it produced confiderable effect on the audience.

It was a matter of concern, to judges of theatrical merit, to fee fuch actors as Booth and Powell condemned to reprefent the inferior parts of Banquo and Lenox, when Mills was fo improperly fet over their heads. Roberts the player, author of a letter to Mr. Pope concerning fome paffages in his preface to Shakfpeare, told me that the indignation of a country gentleman broke out one night, during the acting of this play, in a very odd manner. The 'fquire, after having been heartily tired with Mills, on the appearance of his old companion, George Powell, in the fourth act, cried out, loud enough to be heard by the audience, ' For God's fake, George, give me a fpeech and let me go home.'

Quin's figure and countenance, in this character, fpoke much in his favour; but he was deficient in animated utterance, and wanted flexibility of tone. He could neither affume the ftrong agitation of mind before the murder of the king, nor the remorfe and anguifh in confequence of it:—much lefs could he put on that mixture of defpair, rage, and frenzy, that mark the laft fcenes of Macbeth. During the whole reprefentation he fcarce ever deviated from a dull, heavy, monotony.

Moffop's power of expreffion, in feveral fituations of Macbeth, commanded attention and applaufe. Had he been acquainted with variety of action

action and easy deportment, he would have been justly admired in it. Barry ought never to have attempted that which was so opposite to his natural manner. He was not formed to represent the terrible agonies of Macbeth.

The genius of a Garrick could alone comprehend and execute the complicated passions of this character. From the first scene, in which he was accosted by the witches to the end of the part, he was animated and consistent. The tumult raised in his mind, by the prophecy of the witches, was expressed by feelings suitable to the occasion, nor did he suffer the marks of this agitation to be entirely dissipated in the presence of Duncan, which he discovered to the audience in no obscure manner; more especially when the king named Malcolm prince of Cumberland.

Before I conclude my account of the several actors who personated Macbeth, I must take notice of a piece of stage perfidy which had like to have produced disagreeable consequences to a performer of that character.

Oliver Cashel was by birth an Irishman, well educated, and of a good family. His inclination to the profession of acting brought him first to the stage of Drury lane, and afterwards to that of Covent-Garden, where he met with such encouragement from Mr. Rich, that he excited the jealousy of an actor who had been for a considerable time advancing equally in the favour of the manager. Cashel was bred in high tory principles, which he took no pains to conceal, but indiscreetly threw out his notions of government and political affairs in mixed companies. The man was innocent of any intention to disturb the state;

he

he was only rash in the use of expressions which might be interpreted to his disadvantage. The nation was, in 1746, involved in a French and Spanish war, and a rebellion had broken out in Scotland. The rival of Cashel, though not known by him to be such, took advantage of his unguarded warmth of temper, and secretly laid an information against him at the secretary of state's office. The accused person was taken up by a general warrant, and examined by the secretary of state. Nothing worthy the notice of government appearing in his disfavour, he was set at liberty. The first place he resorted to was the Bedford Coffee-house, where he found his secret and perfidious enemy waiting the issue of his information. Cashel was going very innocently to relate his unexpected adventure to him; but the other, shocked at his sight, ran out of the coffee-house in great haste, to shun the man whom he had so basely endeavoured to injure. Soon after this transaction, news arrived from Scotland of the battle of Falkirk, where, it was supposed, the rebels had gained some slight advantage. The king was advised to go to the theatre, and to command the tragedy of Macbeth. Cashel's examination before a minister of state was known to the public, and Rich doubted whether it would be prudent to permit him to act the principal character before the king. Quin heard of the manager's scruples, and offered his service without any expectation of reward. But the king being asked if he had any objection to Mr. Cashel's acting before him, answered, "By no means, he would be altogether as acceptable as any other player." A few months after, Cashel

was

was seized with an apoplectic fit, as he was acting on the stage at Norwich, which he did not long survive; his enemy died, I believe, much about the same time.

CHAP. XXVII.

Banquo's description of Duncan's complacency.—Macbeth's drink.—The meaning of the word wines.—*Dagger-scene.—Duke of Parma and David Garrick.——Quotation from Æschylus.——Tarquin's strides.—Connoisseur and Garrick.—Lady Macbeth works herself to the encouragement of murder.—By what methods.—*Say their prayers, and most need of Blessing, *explained.—Quotation from the hymns of Orpheus and the Choæphoræ of Æschylus.—The play of Macbeth an admirable sermon against murder.—Excellence of Garrick and Pritchard.—Short hose of the French.—Story of Nokes.—Mrs. Porter.—Direction to the actor of Macduff.—*Unmannerly *explained.—*Breech'd, *from Massinger.—*Naked faculties, *note upon—Loud grief to be suppressed.—Behaviour of the actors in a scene after the king's murder.—King Duffus.—Donald and his wife.—Perfect spy of the time.—Lady Macbeth's discontent.—Melancholy state of the murderer.—*Dearest chuck *explained.—Feast sold.—Ghost of Banquo.—Lloyd's verses.—Garrick's opinion of the merit of Macbeth.—Garrick and Mrs. Pritchard.—Their various excellences.—Quotation from Æschylus.—*Young in deed.—*Pit of Acheron and the brook of Acheneen.---Macbeth and Macduff's mutual jealousy from Buchanan.*

BANQUO.

BANQUO.

——— And shut up
In measureless contentment.

BANQUO's description of Duncan's full enjoyment of his entertainment presents a most amiable picture of a benevolent mind. The words *measureless contentment* give an idea of unbounded goodness and complacency.

MACBETH.

Go bid thy mistress, when my drink is ready, she strike upon the bell.

In the times of the feudal system, kings, princes, barons, and all persons of distinguished birth and rank, before they went to rest, partook of a collation called the *wines,* consisting of delicate cates and wine, warmed and mixed with certain spices. Froissart esteemed it a great piece of good fortune that he spent the greatest part of his life in the courts of princes, for thereby he had gained *an opportunity of drinking the wines, which,* he says, *contributed much to his comfort and repast.** This is the cordial which we may reasonably suppose Shakspeare meant by the drink.

IDEM.

———————————

* Froissart. Tom ii. Chap. 81.

IDEM.

Is this a dagger which I see before me?

Many stage critics suppose this to be one of the most difficult situations in acting. The sudden start on seeing the dagger in the air,---the endeavour of the actor to seize it,---the disappointment,---the suggestion of its being only a vision of the disturbed fancy,---the seeing it still in form most palpable, with the reasoning upon it,------these are difficulties which the mind of Garrick was capable of encountering and subduing. So happy did he think himself in the exhibition of this scene, that, when he was in Italy, and requested by the duke of Parma to give a proof of his skill in action, to the admiration of that prince, he at once threw himself into the attitude of Macbeth's seeing the air-drawn dagger. The duke desired no farther proof of Garrick's great excellence in his profession, being perfectly convinced, by this specimen, that he was an absolute master of it.

IDEM.

————Now o'er one half the world
Nature lies dead, and wicked dreams abuse
The curtain'd sleep.

This is not unlike a passage in the Coœphoræ of Æschylus:

For in the still and midnight hour,
When darkness aids his hideous power,
Affright, that breathes his vengeance deep,
Haunts with wild dreams the curtain'd sleep.
POTTER'S ÆSCHYLUS.

IDEM.

IDEM.

With Tarquin's ravishing *strides.*

Mr. Steevens has, from Spencer and Harrington's Ariosto, brought instances to prove that the word *stride* does not always convey the idea of violent motion. Notwithstanding this, I believe that almost every body, who reads the line as above quoted, will suppose the word to import something like tumult and noise. But all disputes, about the word *strides,* may easily be determined by restoring what, I think, is the genuine reading, *sides,* which was first removed by Mr. Pope, who, in its stead, substituted *strides.* ' I am now, says Macbeth, moving towards my purpose with the cautious steps of the ravishing Tarquin, or the silent pace of a ghost.' The sides of a man, in our language, like the latera or humeri of the Latins, signify his power and ability.

In Twelfth Night, the duke tells Viola,

  ———There is *no woman's sides*
  Can bide the beating of so strong a passion
  As love doth give my heart.

By a very common figure, the sides of a man stand for the man himself.

IDEM.

  ———Hear it not, Duncan, for it is a bell
  That summons thee to heaven or to hell!

The thought is solemn, though, I believe, every reader wishes there had been no chime on an occasion so tremendous. But Davenant lessens the gloom of the idea still farther, by an alteration very improper:

———Hear it not, Duncan, for it is a bell
That rings my coronation and thy knell!

Upon Macbeth's going off the stage to perpetrate the murder, the author of the Connoisseur observes, that the actor's feelings must have been disturbed by his wiping the paint from his face to look more ghastly on his re-entrance, besides the disordering of his wig to give the appearance of bustle and distraction. Would not the same author, if the actor had returned from the supposed murder as unruffled in dress and as florid in look as before, have justly remarked that he had forgotten the situation in which his author had placed him, for he bore no outward signs of a man concerned in the business of assassination? He might as well, too, have remarked that the player must have employed some of his time in dipping the stage-daggers in blood. But there is no end of such criticism; I am sorry that remarks of this kind should escape a writer not more remarkable for candour of spirit than force of genius.

LADY MACBETH.

That, which hath made them drunk, hath made me bold!
What hath quench'd them, hath given me fire!

By these lines being put in the mouth of Lady Macbeth, Shakspeare seems unwilling to suppose that one of the tender sex could be wrought up to become an associate in murder, without some preparation for it, by a degree of intoxication.

MACBETH.

MACBETH.

But they did say their pray'rs, and address'd them
Again to sleep.

By 'saying their prayers,' the author means, they poured out such short addresses to the divine Being as men disturbed by troublesome dreams, or frightened by sudden apprehension of danger, generally ejaculate: such as imploring Heaven's protection, begging forgiveness of sins, and the like. This will give us the true meaning of what Macbeth says immediately after.

MACBETH.

—————I could not say amen,
When they did cry, Heaven bless us!
I had most need of blessing.

Macbeth could not, even in his then distracted state of mind, suppose that heaven would sanctify murder by giving a blessing to the murderer. Blessing is here put for pardon: 'I had most need of forgiveness.'

IDEM.

Macbeth doth murder sleep,—the innocent sleep!—
Sleep that knits up the ravelled sleeve of care,
The death of each day's life, sore labour's bath,
Balm of hurt minds, great nature's second course,
Chief nourisher in life's feast!

These

These attributes of sleep greatly resemble some beautiful lines in the Hymns of Orpheus to Night and Sleep:

Κλυθι, μακαιρα θια,——
Ευφροσυνι τερπνη, φιλοπαννυχι, μητερ ονειρων,
Ληθομεριμν' αγαθη τι, πονων αναπαυσιν εχυσα,——
Νυν τι μακαιρα Νυξ πολυολβιε, πασι ποθεινι, &c.

———————

Υπνε αναξ μακαρων παντων θνητων τ' ανθρωπων,——
Σωματα δεσμευων εν αχαλκευτοισι πεδησι,
Λυσιμεριμνε, κοπων ηδειαν εχων αναπαυσιν,
Και πασης λυπης ιερον παραμυθιον ερδων.

IDEM.

Will all great Neptune's ocean wash this blood
Clean from my hand? No, this my hand will rather
The multitudinous sea incarnadine.

The Chorus, in the Coephoræ of Æschylus, breathes sentiments not unlike this of Macbeth:

———Were all the streams, that wind
  Their mazy progress to the main,
To cleanse this odious stain, in one combin'd,
  The streams combin'd would flow in vain.

Potter's Æschylus.

IDEM.

To know my deed 'twere best not know myself.

' Whilst I am conscious of having committed this murder, I cannot but be miserable; I have no remedy but in the total forgetfulness of the deed, or, to speak more plainly, in the loss of my senses.'

The

The merit of this scene transcends all panegyric. Amongst the many discourses, which, from the earliest time to the present hour, have been composed on the subject of murder, it will be difficult to find so powerful a dissuasive or dehortation from that dreadful crime as the tragedy of Macbeth exhibits. In drawing the principal character of the play, the author has deviated somewhat from history; but, by abating the fierceness of Macbeth's disposition, he has rendered him a fitter subject for the drama. The rational and severe delight, which the spectator feels from the representation of this piece, proceeds, in a great measure, from the sensibility of the murderer, from his remorse and agonies, and from the torments he suffers in the midst of his successful villany.

The representation of this terrible part of the play, by Garrick and Mrs. Pritchard, can no more be described than I believe it can be equalled. I will not separate these performers, for the merits of both were transcendent. His distraction of mind and agonizing horrors were finely contrasted by her seeming apathy, tranquillity, and confidence. The beginning of the scene after the murder was conducted in terrifying whispers. Their looks and action supplied the place of words. You heard what they spoke, but you learned more from the agitation of mind displayed in their action and deportment. The poet here gives only an outline to the consummate actor.——*I have done the deed!*——*Didst thou not hear a noise?*——*When?*——*Did you not speak?* ——The dark colouring, given by the actor to these abrupt speeches, makes the scene awful and tremendous to the auditors! The wonderful expression

pression of heartful horror, which Garrick felt when he shewed his bloody hands, can only be conceived and described by those who saw him! The expression of 'sorry sight!' is certainly not happy now. Words, which were highly expressive and energetic above one hundred and fifty years since, have by length of time, lost their importance.————Davenant, fifty years after, altered *sorry* to *dismal*; but perhaps a better word than that might still be substituted.

PORTER.

Who's there?—Here's an English tailor, come hither for stealing out of a French hose.

The archness of the joke, says Dr. Warburton, consists in the French hose being very short and strait, for that tailor must be master of his trade who could steal any thing thence. Mr. Steevens declares freely, that Dr. Warburton made this objection at random, and quotes an old pamphlet of Stubbs to prove, 'the Gallick hosen are made very large and wide, reaching down to their knees.' Dr. Farmer, in favour of Dr. Warburton, observes that Mr. Steevens had forgotten the uncertainty of French fashions, and quotes from an old book a passage to prove that French hose answered in length to their shortskirted doublets. As a father proof that our neighbours, the French, in the reign of Louis IV. were fond of short doublets, I shall present the reader with a stage-anecdote from honest Downs, the theatrical historian, who relates, 'That when King Charles II. and all his court, met his sister, the Duchess of Orleans, at Dover, the comedy of Sir Solomon Single, acted before both courts,

courts, pleased her grace and all the spectators extremely. The French wore, at the same time, short laced coats, some scarlet, some blue, adorned with broad waist-belts. Nokes had on, in the part of Sir Arthur Addle, one shorter than the rest; the Duke of Monmouth gave him his sword and belt from his side, and buckled it on himself, on purpose to mimic the French. Nokes looked more like a dressed-up ape than a man; so that on his first entrance upon the stage, he put the king and the whole court into an excessive fit of laughter; at which, the French were very chagrined to see themselves aped by such a fool as Sir Arthur. Mr. Nokes kept the duke's sword to his dying day.'

MACDUFF.

——— Up, up, and see
The great doom's image!

'A picture of horror not to be paralleled but in the universal ruin of the world at the last day.'

LADY MACBETH.

What's the business?

The players have long since removed Lady Macbeth from this scene. A London audience we may suppose not to be so critical as that of Athens, or such an one as Oxford or Cambridge could supply.——— Many years since, I have been informed, an experiment was hazarded, whether the spectators would bear Lady Macbeth's surprize and fainting; but, however characterisracteriſtical ſuch behaviour might be, perſons of a certain claſs were ſo merry upon the occaſion, that it was not thought proper to venture the Lady's appearance any more. Mr. Garrick thought, that even ſo favourite an actreſs as Mrs. Pritchard would not, in that ſituation, eſcape deriſion from the gentlemen in the upper regions. Mr. Macklin is of opinion, that Mrs. Porter alone could have credit with an audience, to induce them to endure the hypocriſy of Lady Macbeth.

MACBETH.

O, yet I do repent me of my fury
That I did kill them.

MACDUFF.

————Why did you ſo?

The murder of Duncan's chamber-grooms, by Macbeth, juſtly raiſes ſuſpicion in Macduff. I have ſeldom ſeen an actor of this character, who rightly underſtood his ſituation: his eye ought to purſue and examine Macbeth's demeanor during the remainder of the ſcene, though not in ſuch a manner as to diſcover what paſſed in his mind to the ſuſpected perſon.

MACBETH.

Unmannerly breech'd with gore.

Propriety of expreſſion was not the principal ſtudy of Shakſpeare. He frequently lays hold of the firſt word that meets his fancy; though I ſee no reason to cavil with *unmannerly*, which Mr.ʳ Warton supports very forcibly. The word, with compounds of the same import, are in good authors to be found in a sense not very remote from this in Shakspeare. In Dryden, *unmannered* signifies uncivil, rude, and brutal; *unmannerliness*, in Locke, is indecent behaviour and breach of civility. *Unmannerly*, in this quotation, means indecently in the highest degree! brutally! shockingly!———The propriety of the word *unmannerly*, in this place, may be justified by a like freedom taken by Greek and Latin authors in words seemingly as remote from their original meaning:—Dr. Clarke in a learned note upon Αλγησας δ' αχρειον ιδων, in the second book of Homer's Iliad, l. 279, observes, that αχρειον ιδων elegantissime dictum est, et tam significanter ut nil possit supra. Latine dicens *inutile tuens*, sicuti *torvum tuens*, &c. Observandum autem αχρειος apud Græcos, quum de homine malo dicitur, non utique eum exhibere qui simpliciter sit *non utilis*, sed qui sit *maxime nequam*. Similiter apud optimos linguæ Romanæ auctores, inutile legitur id, non quod non utile modo, *sed quicquid utili maxime est contrarium*. The whole note I would recommend to the perusal of the candid and judicious reader.

Dr. Warburton's *reech'd*, instead of *breech'd*, is plausible; but the old reading is well justified by Mr. Steevens, and still more forcibly by Dr. Farmer. *Breech'd* was certainly a common word, in our author's time, applied to the covering of any thing, as well as a part of a man's body. Sometimes it signifies the direct contrary, as in Massinger's Guardian, act I. Durazzo, speaking of
his

his nephew's distant and bashful courtship of his mistress:

> How he looks like a school-boy that had play'd
> The truant, and went to be *breech'd*.

BANQUO.

> And, when we have our naked faculties hid,
> Which suffer in exposure———

In such a cloud of words, Mr. Steevens is afraid lest the meaning should escape the reader; and therefore he informs them, that they are to understand by them,———'*When we have clothed our half-dressed bodies, which may take cold from being exposed to the air.*' Shakspeare understood not only the propriety and decorum of the stage, but the genius of his audience, and would never send on his characters half dressed. Such a ludicrous sight, which no skill could prevent, would have excited loud bursts of laughter. This appearance certainly would be very natural; for the ringing of a bell, and a loud outcry of murder, must, in a palace, or any house, have drawn together the highest and lowest of its inmates, some armed with one weapon, some with another: but, at such a motley sight, surely,

> To be grave exceeds all power of face.

In the more advanced state of the stage, Mr. Garrick would not risk the appearance of half, or even disordered, dress, though extremely proper, and what the incident of the fable and situation of the characters seemed to require. But the words will, I think, very easily bear another meaning: '*When we have recovered ourselves from that grief and those transports of passion,*
which,

which, though justifiable from natural feeling and the sad occasion, do but expose the frailty and imbecility of our nature.'

Extreme grief and loud lamentations, however natural, and to be indulged in private, are surely not graceful in public, and are always there endeavoured to be suppressed. Our Shakspeare is very careful to restrain excessive grief in the presence of others. In Julius Cæsar, act III. the servant of Octavius, on seeing the dead body of Cæsar, cries 'O Cæsar!' and bursts into tears: Mark Antony checks his sorrow, in that place, by saying, 'Thy heart is full; *get thee apart and weep.*' And Kent, in King Lear, act IV. describing Cordelia's behaviour, when told of the cruelty of her sisters to her father:

———————Then she shook
The holy water from her heav'nly eyes,
And clamour moisten'd her.—Then away she started,
To deal with grief alone.

MACBETH.

Let's briefly put on manly readiness,
And meet in the hall together.

This scene of strong perturbation and deep sorrow requires, in the representation, the nicest and most accurate management.—The guilty Macbeth, though struggling to assume the appearance of innocence and deep concern, dares not meet the eye of any person. The rest walk up and down as if sighing and lamenting; only Macduff and the sons of Duncan seem, by their looks, to point out the murderer.

ROSS.

―――――By the clock 'tis day,
And yet dark night ſtrangles the travelling lamp.—
—Darkneſs doth the face of earth entomb,
When living light ſhould kiſs it.

From the hiſtory of King Duffus's murder, by Donald, governor of the citadel of Foris, Shakſpeare has borrowed ſome incidents and ſome embelliſhments for his fable. Duffus, having determined to bring to juſtice ſome robbers, who had laid waſte Murray, Roſs, and Caithneſs, cauſed them to be ſeized and brought to Foris, there to receive condign puniſhment. Donald was greatly offended that the king would not be prevailed upon to pardon ſome friends of his aſſociated in the robberies. His wife, who, in violence of diſpoſition, greatly reſembles Lady Macbeth, ſtimulated her huſband to murder the king from the conveniency of doing it; for, having the command of the caſtle, ſhe told him, he had the power of executing the deſign in his own hands. This, I take it, is Shakſpeare's *time and place agreeing*. Mr. Steevens has already produced the tale of the hawk and the mouſing owl from the ſame ſource with the killing of Duffus's grooms.*

The

---

* Something, ſimilar to this ſtory of the hawk and mouſing owl, we read in the Perſæ of Æſchylus.

    ALOSSA.—An eagle I beheld
Fly to the altar of the ſun :—aghaſt
I ſtood, my friends, and ſpeechleſs; when a hawk
With eager ſpeed runs thither, furious cuffs
The eagle with his wings, and with his talons,
Unplumes his head : mean time th'imperial bird
Cow'rs to the blows, defenceleſs.—Potter's Æſchylus.

The description of darkness obscuring the hemisphere, by Ross, is borrowed from the same history. Buchanan says, indeed there was a general darkness, over all Scotland, after the murder of Duffus, that neither sun nor moon were to be seen for the space of six months after.

Act III. Scene I.

MACBETH.

Acquaint you with the perfect spy of the time.

Dr. Johnson thinks, by the *perfect spy* is meant the third Murderer, whom Macbeth sends to join the other two. But one of the two first who were employed did not so understand it, by questioning the third. 'The perfect spy of the time' is well explained by the words which follow, 'the moment of it', that is, the very instant you are to begin your bloody business. At the same time the King dismisses them, commanding them to stay within till he calls them. The sending a third murdering assistant is an after-thought, proceeding from Macbeth's anxious impatience to have the business finished.

LADY MACBETH.

—————Nought's had, all's spent,
Where our desire is got without content.
'Tis safer to be that which we destroy,
Than, by destruction, dwell in doubtful joy.

The Lady is willing to enjoy the fruits of the abominable crime which her husband, by her instigation and assistance, had committed; but, seeing discontent lay hold of his mind, and all their hopes of happiness abortive, she now begins to think it would be safer, that is, in our author's intention, *more eligible*, to be the murdered than the murderer. She was approaching to that state of mind which is so beautifully described in the Tempest, where the good Gonsalvo, speaking of Alonzo and his guilty associates, says,

—————— Their great guilt,
Like poison giv'n to work a great time after,
Now 'gins to bite their spirits.

LADY MACBETH.

—————— Why do you keep alone.
Of *sorriest fancies* your companions making?

'Sorriest fancies' do not here, as Dr. Johnson imagines, signify worthless, ignoble, and vile, imaginations; but, doubtless, black, gloomy, and melancholy, reflections. Mr. Steevens admits, that *sorriest* may possibly mean melancholy and dismal, and quotes a passage from the Comedy of Errors to prove it; but he needed not have gone so far; as Macbeth, after committing the murder on Duncan, makes use of the word *sorry* in that sense: for, shewing his hands, in an agony he cries out, 'This is a *sorry* sight!' this is a sight not to be viewed without horror!

MACBETH.

MACBETH.

──────── Unsafe the while that we
Must lave our honours in these flattering streams,
And make our faces vizards to our hearts.

Happy it is for the world, that the villain can seldom quietly and peaceably enjoy the fruits of his iniquity. He, who before found dissimulation and flattery his best conductors to the throne, is now surfeited with, and loathes, them. But *safer* signifies here, as in the preceding soliloquy of the Lady, *preferable.* He intends, by the word *unsafe,* likewise to express the disagreeable tenure by which he holds his life and crown, by being obliged to soothe and flatter those whom he mortally hates.

IDEM.

Be innocent of the knowledge, dearest *chuck.*

Chuck, from *chick,* or *chicken;* or perhaps a word of fondness borrowed from the hen, who invites her little brood to partake of what she has scratched from the ground, and emits a sound resembling *chuck* or *cluck.* Othello, act III. makes use of the same term:

What promise, *chuck?*

Scene IV. Banquet.

LADY MACBETH.

──────── The feast is sold
That is not often vouch'd while it is making.

'If you do not give due welcome to your guests, by paying them proper attention, the feast will resemble a dinner at an inn, or ordinary, where every man pays for his share of the entertainment.'

The Ghost of Banquo rises, and sits in Macbeth's chair.

It has been questioned, whether Banquo's ghost should not present itself to the imagination of Macbeth, as the dagger did before the murder of the King. The appearance of a ghost is thought by some a mere trick, a *jeu du théâtre*; and Lloyd, in his excellent poem of the Actor, has ridiculed, in very animated lines, the mealy appearance of Banquo:

> When chilling horrors shake th'affrighted King,
> And guilt torments him with her scorpion-sting;
> When keenest feelings at his bosom pull,
> And fancy tells him that the seat is full;
> Why need the ghost usurp the monarch's place,
> To frighten children with his mealy face?
> The king alone should form the phantom there,
> And talk and tremble at the empty chair.

It must be confessed, these visionary appearances are but helps to the unaccomplished actor and the ignorant spectator. Nothing can be pleaded in their behalf but prescriptive right, the constant practice of the theatre. Shakspeare lived in the infancy of the stage, when a rude audience demanded all the assistance which the poet could give them. He may be justified for calling up the spirit of Banquo, to raise feelings in the actor and

and terror in the spectator; but it is now time to try, at least, what effect may be produced without such ghostly aid.

Before Mr. Garrick displayed the terrible graces of action from the impression of visionary appearance, the comedians were strangers to the effects which this scene could produce. Macbeth, they constantly exclaimed, was not a character of the first rate; all the pith of it was exhausted, they said, in the first and second acts of the play. They formed their judgment from the drowsy and ineffectual manner of Garrick's predecessors, who could not force attention or applause from the audience during the three last acts. When Roscius was informed what judgment the players had conceived of Macbeth, he smiled, and said, he should be very unhappy if he were not able to keep alive the attention of the spectators to the last syllable of so animated a character.

This admirable scene was greatly supported by the speaking terrors of Garrick's look and action. Mrs. Pritchard shewed admirable art in endeavouring to hide Macbeth's frenzy from the observation of the guests, by drawing their attention to conviviality. She smiled on one, whispered to another, and distantly saluted a third; in short, she practised every possible artifice to hide the transaction that passed between her husband and the vision his disturbed imagination had raised. Her reproving and angry looks, which glanced towards Macbeth, at the same time were mixed with marks of inward vexation and uneasiness. When, at last, as if unable to support her feelings any longer, she rose from her seat, and seized his

his arm, and, with a half-whisper of terror, said, 'Are you a man!' she assumed a look of such anger, indignation, and contempt, as cannot be surpassed.

MACBETH.

It will have blood, they say; blood will have blood!

So in the Coœphoræ of Æschylus:

There is a law, that, for each drop of blood
Shed on the earth, demands that blood be shed.
POTTER'S ÆSCHYLUS.

IDEM.

——————— My strange and self abuse
Is the initiate fear that wants hard use:
We are but young in deed.

This is one, amongst a thousand other instances, of our author's great knowledge of nature. The criminal agent, when he has recovered from the terrors of his afflicted conscience, rushes headlong into more guilt, by attributing his fears to any thing, except the real cause of them. Macbeth pacifies himself with this cordial, that his internal alarms are all owing to novelty of practice, and that persisting in evil would alone procure repose to his mind and stability to his government. So says Richard III.

Things bad begun make strong themselves by ill.

Scene V.

————— Get you gone,
And meet me in the pit of Acheron.

Shakspeare, says Mr. Steevens, thought it allowable to bestow the name of Acheron on any fountain, lake, or pit, through which there was supposed to be a communication between that river and the infernal regions; but Shakspeare, I believe, did not know that, in the woods of Calder or Cawdor, there was a brook very near in name to that of the hellish river. ' For, within those woods, says Mr. Pennant, there are deep rocky glens, darkened with trees round each side of the wood; one has a great torrent roaring at its bottom, called the *brook of Acheneen:* it well merits the name of Acheron; being a most fit scene for witches to celebrate their nocturnal rites in.'*

Scene VI. Lenox and another lord.

This scene is left out in representation, supposed to be unnecessary to the plot of the play.

LENOX.

————— Did he not strait,
In pious rage, the two delinquents tear
That were the slaves of drink and thralls of fear?

Lenox.

* Pennant's Tour to Scotland, P. 124.

Lenox was present when Macbeth killed the sleeping grooms, and, however better instructed he seems to be at present, he then justified the act, from the bloody daggers lying unwiped upon the pillows, and from their staring and distracted looks; at the same time, saying,

>No man's life was to be trusted with them.

IDEM.

>———For, from broad hints and cause, he fail'd
>His presence at the tyrant's feast, I hear
>Macduff lives in disgrace.

The story of Macduff and the tyrant's mutual jealousy is related, after this manner, by Buchanan:

'For his better security, Macbeth was resolved to build a castle on the high hill of Dunsinane, and to fortify it very strongly. He summoned the thanes to assist in erecting the fortifications by turns. Macduff suspected the king harboured some evil intentions towards him, and, though he sent abundance of materials and labourers, with certain friends to quicken their operations, yet he would not attend in person. Macbeth, one day inspecting the works, observed that a team of oxen, sent by Macduff, was unequal to the task of reaching the summit of the hill: upon this he took occasion to say, that he was no stranger to the thane's contumacy and disobedience, which he was determined to conquer, by fixing a yoke upon his own neck. Macduff, as soon as he was informed of this, immediately hired a veſſel, and ſet ſail to Lothian, and from thence he ſet out for England.'

CHAP.

CHAP. XXVIII.

Incantation of witches.—Jonson's contention with Shakspeare.—Quotations from his Queen's Masque.—Speech of Macbeth to the presiding bags.—Invocation.—Hecate.—Attire of Jonson's witches.—King's evil.—Why confined to them.—Claim of the French kings from Clovis.—Queen-consorts never touched for the evil.—Lewis XI. *and St. Francis of Paul, their meeting.—Banishment of royal witchcraft.—Macduff's character.—Wilks, Booth, and Ryan.—*Hell is murky *explained.—English epicures.—Old enmity between the English and Scots.—Juvenal quoted.—Deportment of Macduff criticised.—Title of Thane, from Spelman, Buchanan, and Gurdon.*

Act IV. Scene I.

FIRST WITCH.

Thrice the brinded cat hath mew'd.

THE incantation, in this act, has been greatly celebrated, and, for boldness of invention, strength of imagination, and propriety of conduct, is thought equal to any effort of our author's genius.

Mr. Malone has, with much probability, fixed the first representation of Macbeth to the year 1606. However that may be, we are certain it was acted before Ben Jonson produced his Masque of Queens, which was exhibited before the king and

and queen in 1609. In that compofition there are many evident imitations of the magical inchantment in Macbeth. The fuccefs of Shakfpeare alarmed the jealoufy of a man who fancied himfelf his rival, or rather his fuperior. In this mafque, Jonfon has meafured fwords with our inimitable poet, and, to be juft, we muft own he has difplayed abundance of reading, and no mean vein of poetry. But, left I fhould fall under the charge of afferting what I cannot prove, I will prefent the reader with fome extracts from the Mafque, in which the imitator endeavours, though in vain, to conceal his obligations to the original.

Twelve hags bring their dame, who is fubftituted in the place of Hecate, an account of the ingredients which they have gathered to make the charm powerful. She fees them bufy, and cries out, almoft in the words of Shakfpeare, ' Well done, my hags !' She bids them relate what they have done.

FIRST HAG.

I have been all day looking after
A raven feeding upon a quarter.
As foon fhe turn'd her beak to the fouth,
I fnatch'd this morfel out of her mouth.

SECOND HAG.

I have been gathering wolves hairs,
The mad dog's foam, and the adder's ears.
The fpurging of a dead man's eyes,
And all fince the evening-ftar did rife.

SIXTH WITCH.

I had a dagger, what did I with that?
Kill'd an infant to have his fat.

TENTH.

I from the jaws of a gardener's bitch,
Did snatch these bones, and then leapt a ditch.

ELEVENTH.

I went to the toad lives under the wall;
I charm'd him out, and he came to my call.
I scratch'd out the eyes of the owl before;
I tore the bat's wing: what have you more?

I shall close my proofs with two quotations more. The abrupt, but sublime, address of Macbeth to the witches, in this fourth act; and an imitation of it spoken by the dame in the Masque. The merit of both will plead in their behalf.

MACBETH.

How now, you secret, black, and midnight hags!
I conjure you, by that which you profess,
Howe'er you come to know it, answer me;
Though you untie the winds, and let them fight
Against the churches: though the yesty waves
Confound and swallow navigation up;
Though bladed corn be lodg'd and trees blown:
Though castles topple on their warders heads:
Though palaces and pyramids do slope
Their heads to their foundations: though the treasure
Of nature's germins tumble all together,
E'en till destruction sicken—Answer me.
To what I ask you!

The

MACBETH. 113

The dame's invocation, from Jonson.

You fiends and furies, if yet any be
Worse than ourselves, you that have quak'd to see
These knots unty'd, and shrunk when we have charm'd.
You, that, to arm us, have yourselves disarm'd,
And to our pow'rs refign'd your whips and brands,
When we went forth the scourge of men and lands.
You that have seen me ride when Hecate
Durst not take chariot; when the boisterous sea,
Without a breath of wind, hath knock'd the sky,
And that hath thunder'd, Jove not knowing why.
When we have set the elements at wars,
Made midnight see the sun, and day the stars.
When the wing'd light'ning in the course hath staid,
And swiftest rivers have run back, afraid
To see the corn remove, the groves to range,
Whole places alter, and the seasons change:
When the pale moon, at the first voice, down fell,
Poison'd, and durst not stay the second spell—
You that have oft been conscious of these fights,
And thou, thrice-formed star, that on these nights,
Art only powerful, to whose triple name
Thus we incline, once, twice, and thrice, the same,
If now with rites profane and foul enough
We do invoke thee, darken all the roof,
With present fogs exhale earth's rott'nest vapours,
And strike a blindness thro' these blazing tapers, &c.

Notwithstanding Jonson, in the composition of this invocation, had the assistance of the antient poets whom he cites in his margin, it is little more than an amplification, or extended paraphrase, of the speech of Macbeth which I have just quoted. The word Hecate, which Shakspeare abridges to two syllables, Jonson, to shew his learning, restores to its ancient measure. The exordium of this piece, called the Masque of Queens, celebrated from the house of fame, is very curious: 'His majesty being set, and the whole company in full expectation, *the part of the scene which first presented itself was an ugly hell, which, flaming beneath, smoked to the top of the roof.*' This was beating Shakspear's cauldron with a witness. The Witches were all differently attired; some with rats on their heads, some on their shoulders; others with ointment-pots at their girdles; all with spindles, timbrels, rattles, or other veneficial instruments, making a confused noise, with strange gestures. The incantations of Shakspeare, it is observed, are awfully tremendous; those of other poets generally ridiculous.

Scene III.

MALCOLM.

Let us seek out some desolate shade.

Mr. Steevens has quoted Hollingshead's abridgment of a long discourse between Malcolm and Macduff, from H. Boetius, on which this scene is founded. I think he might have shortened the margin very much, by transcribing Buchanan, who agrees with his countryman in the subject of the dialogue, but is more succinct in the relation.

MALCOLM.

MALCOLM.

Why in that rawnefs left your wife and child?

The King, in Hamlet, Act IV. condemns his own conduct, in privately burying Polonius, in words of the fame import:

We have done but greenly.

DOCTOR.

——— There are a crew of wretched fouls
That ſtay his cure.———
————————At his touch,
Such fanctity hath heaven given his hand,
They prefently amend.

As the poet here intended a compliment to his royal mafter, it is moſt probable, that King James had, before the acting of this play, touched for the king's evil; nor can we fuppofe he would long defer affuming this power inherent in his predeceffors.

The privilege of curing the king's evil is attributed only to kings. No other fovereigns, of any degree, have laid claim to it. Why not give this power, fays Voltaire, to emperors? and indeed, a fortiori, why is it not refident in the popes? they are fomething more than God's images upon earth; they are his vicars, his vicegerents. The fame author fuppofes, that fome vifionary, in order to make the baſtaɪdy of William the conqueror more refpectable, beſtowed on him, as a gift from heaven, the power to cure the evil by a touch.

The

The kings of France could not, without a jealous eye, behold this extraordinary gift of celestial power in an English king, without putting in their claim to a similar influence. It was therefore pretended, that they also, from their ancestor, King Clovis, enjoyed the like gift of curing the king's evil.

Queen consorts never pretended to this prerogative of the royal touch, because their hands, it seems, were not anointed like those of the kings; but Queen Elizabeth, being a sovereign in her own right, cured those, who were afflicted with this distemper, with great facility. It was happy for his subjects, that Lewis XI. of France, was not a free thinker; his avarice, tyranny, and oppression, would then, perhaps, have been unlimited; but his gross superstition was a check to his more dangerous vices, and the fear of damnation, in all probability, saved many an innocent life. Lewis, in order to remove the consequences of an apoplexy, sent for a famous man, called St. Francis of Paul, to cure him. Behold, when the saint arrived, he was terribly afflicted with the king's evil. Here Lewis had an opportunity to do one good turn for another; but it appeared, to all the world, that the king could neither cure the saint nor the saint the king. The courtiers, if they durst, would have loudly laughed at them both.

The house of Brunswick renounced all pretensions to royal witchcraft; they claim no power of curing any distemper, by touch of hand, except avarice and ambition. Mr. Nichols, in his very entertaining notes to the anecdotes of Mr. Bowyer, has given, from undisputed authority,
the

the origin of this imposture, which cost some of our princes 3000l. per annum. Queen Elizabeth was so pestered with evil patients in her progress through Gloucestershire, that she honestly told them, 'that God alone could relieve their complaints.' Our pious Charles II. touched no less than 92107 patients, between May 1661 and April 1682.*———Vide Anecdotes of Bowyer, p. 200.

MACDUFF.

He has no children!———

If unshaken loyalty, intrepidity of mind, and tenderness of heart, all united in an eminent degree, can distinguish a character, with submission to Dr. Johnson, Macduff is by these qualities highly discriminated from others. He is indeed, a proper contrast to Macbeth, whose courage degenerates into frenzy.

We are told, by Colley Cibber, that Wilks had once an intention to resign the part of Macduff, in which he had been much applauded, to an inferior actor, and that Booth had made an exchange of Banquo, for this superior character; but that the jealousy of Booth's abilities had caused Wilks to resume what he had so indiscreetly given away. In the strong expression of horror on the murder of the King, and the loud exclamations of surprize and terror, Booth might have exceeded the utmost efforts of Wilks. But, in the touches of domestic woe which require the feelings of the tender father

and

---

* At a guinea a touch, this would amount to a pretty large sum; and hence we see the origin of this costly trick.

and the affectionate husband, Wilks had no equal. His skill, in exhibiting the emotions of the overflowing heart with corresponding look and action, was universally admired and felt. His rising after the suppression of his anguish, into ardent and manly resentment, was highly expressive of noble and generous anger.

We must not forget Ryan's Macduff.--- In the representation of this part, he had nothing to struggle with, but the harshness of his voice. He assumed such genuine terror and amazement, in the second act, as became the actor who was to impose on the spectator a belief of his having seen his royal master murdered! In the 4th act, he felt the loss of his wife and children as became a father and a husband. Ryan, we must own, was inferior to Wilks, but not in a degrading distance.

MALCOLM.

> ———— ————Macbeth
> Is ripe for shaking, and the powers above
> Put on their instruments.

This passage is not, I think, well understood by Mr. Steevens, who interprets it, 'the heavenly powers encourage or thrust forward their mortal instruments.' But the author had a sublimer meaning in this noble image: for it means,

> Heaven itself is arming in our cause.

In the same sense says Richard II.

> For, every man, that Bolingbroke hath prest
> To lift shrewd steel against our golden crown,
> Heaven, for his Richard, hath, in heavenly pay,
> A glorious angel,
>   Richard II. Act 3.

A simi-

A similar thought we find in the supplicants of Æschylus, from the Chorus, speaking of the inscrutable power and wisdom of Jove.

> Though in majesty enthron'd,
> Thick clouds, and dark, inclose him round,
> As from the tower of heaven his eye
> Surveys bold man's impiety;
> Till his ripe wrath on judgment bent,
> He arms each god for punishment,
> And from his high and awful throne,
> Sends all his awful judgment down.
>
> Potter's Æschylus, Vol. I. p. 98.

Act V. Scene I.

Lady Macbeth walking in her sleep.

LADY MACBETH.

Hell is murky!

Mr. Steevens supposes the Lady is talking to Macbeth, and here repeats this expression as if it had come from him, in contempt of his cowardice! for, says he, she would not have even hinted the terrors of hell to one whose conscience she saw was too much alarmed already for her purpose. This is certainly very ingenious; but, if we tread the ground over again, we shall find, that, in reasoning about committing the murder of the King, the fear of hell had no weight with Macbeth. He says positively, that if, without the risk of retaliation, he could accomplish the murder, he would hazard all fear of future retribution, *he would jump the life to come*. But, though

though the murderer scorned to take the future world into his consideration, his Lady might think seriously of the pains of hell. Why else does she say, ' Out, damned spot!' why so pathetically speak of ' the smell of blood!' and tell us, that all the perfumes of Arabia will not ' sweeten her little hand!' and with ' a deep-fetched sigh!' To reason consequentially upon what escapes from a person, disturbed in imagination and distracted with guilt, is not an easy task: but, if we must apply, in this case, to sober argument, ' Hell is murky' would be a natural and fearful suggestion to one who had committed the worst of crimes, and had not quarrelled with her creed. The scene is composed of disjointed thoughts and unconnected ideas, like the picture of a storm, by a great master, where the wreck is variously scattered to shew its terrible effects.

Scene II.

LENOX.

——There is Siward's son,
And many unrough youths that even now
Protest their first of manhood.

Something very similar to this we read in Richard II. act the 3d, in Scrope's speech to the King:

——Boys, with womens voices,
Strive to speak big, and clasp their female joints
In stiff unwieldy arms against thy crown.

Scene

Scene III.

MACBETH.

————Then fly, falfe thanes,
And mingle with the Englifh epicures.

It is an old obfervation, that England is one great cook's fhop; and our neighbours muft confefs, that in no other country are the means of gratifying the appetite to be obtained fo plentifully. To a traveller, in England, no fights prefent themfelves fo frequently to his view as a variety of large convenient inns, and houfes that furnifh good entertainment. Not to contradict any of the commentators, whofe remarks on this paffage are very reafonable, I fhall only obferve, that Macbeth lays hold of the vulgar prejudices of his countrymen, againft their fouthern neighbours, to ferve his prefent purpofe. The reproach of *epicures*, in plainer terms, *Englifh poke-pudding tikes*, or *Englifh bag-pudding dogs*, is as old, I believe, as the enmity between the two nations, and one which the lower clafs, of vulgar Scots, ufed to throw on the Englifh. The frequent fkirmifhes, between the borderers of both kingdoms, ferved to keep alive that hateful animofity which the union itfelf could fcarcely extinguifh. The diverfions of children were expreffive of national ftrife. The young Scots had formerly a game called Englifhmen and Scotchmen: one fide was called Scotch, and the other Englifh. They took off their upper garments, and laid them feverally in heaps; that fide, which plundered the other of moft clothes, won the game.

This

This indeed was particularly expressive of the war, for booty, carried on near the borders.

The English were a match for their neighbours in illiberal taunts and scurrilous reproaches, from which even our parliament was not entirely free; for, when James I. proposed to unite the two kingdoms, several members of the lower house treated his offer in terms of the most significant contempt. In a sarcastic speech, which Osborne has preserved, the Scots were termed, ' sons of the locusts, and daughters of the horse-leech.'

The Ombi and Tentyritæ, two nations of Egypt, were not more averse from one another, on account of the former loving crocodiles, and the other hating them, than the English and Scots were, perhaps for a reason equally ridiculous.

> Inter finitimos vetus atque antiqua simultas,
> Immo tale odium et nunquam sanabile vulnus,
> Ardet adhuc, Ombos et Tentyra: summus utrinque
> Inde furor vulgo, quod numina vicinorum
> Odit uterque locus, cum solos credat habendos
> Esse deos quos ipse colit.
>
> Juvenal. Sat. 15.

MACBETH.

―――― She should have died hereafter;
There would have been a time for such a word!

Macbeth's confidence of victory, in the ensuing contest with Malcolm, was raised to the highest pitch, by the prophecies of Birnam-wood and his not being to be slain by one that was born of woman. In consequence of this opinion, he seems to wish that his Lady had died at a more quiet and less busy time than the present.――――

'There would have been a time for such a word,' is spoken in the same sense with that which Brutus speaks over the dead body of Cassius: 'Cassius, I shall find time, I shall find time.' 'Had she died after my victory, I could then have paid that respect to her memory which I ought.' This explanation is, in general, I believe, conformable to that of Dr. Johnson on the same passage.

IDEM.

And that which should accompany old age,
As honour, love, obedience, troops of friends,
I must not look to have!

Dr. Johnson thinks the courage of Macbeth preserves some esteem; but that quality he had in common with Banquo and others. I am of opinion, that his extreme reluctance to murder his royal master, his uncommon affliction of mind after he had perpetrated the crime, with the perpetual revolt of his conscience upon the commission of each new act of cruelty, are the qualities which render Macbeth, though not worthy of our esteem, yet an object not entirely unmeriting our pity, in spite of his ambition and cruelty.

MACBETH.

'—————Fear not, till Birnam-wood
Do come to Dunsinane.

Birnam-wood, says Mr. Pennant, seems not to have recovered the march of its ancestors to Dunsinane; but there are still to be seen some remains of Macbeth's castle on this high hill.

Scene VI.

MACDUFF.

Make all our trumpets speak, give them all breath.

This and the following line seem to be allotted to Macduff purely to support his consequence; for, according to the rules of propriety, the commanding officer, Malcolm, should have given this charge.

The most difficult part an actor has to sustain, consists in proper action, look, and deportment, when he does not speak. I scarcely remember to have seen any exhibitor of Macduff who had not entirely forgotten, by the tranquility and tameness of his behaviour, the storm which had shaken his whole frame in the preceding act. This is his first appearance after the sad information of his murdered wife and children: should he not, by his look, convince the spectators that he had not lost the remembrance of all that was dear to him? should not his countenance be impressed with grief and resentment; nay, with impatience, too, to take revenge on the man who had so sensibly injured him? Wilks was the only Macduff I can recollect who seemed to have a tolerable notion of his situation; nor indeed did *he,* in deportment, answer the idea of what he should feel on the occasion.

MALCOLM.

————My *thanes* and kinsmen,
Henceforth be earls.

The title of *thane* was not confined to Scotland, but common to the southern, as well as northern, part of the island.———' *Thanorum* appellatio in usu fuit post adventum Normanorum, ut a Domesday liqueat,' says Spelman in his Glossary.———Lesly, de Origine Moribus, &c. Scotorum, has the following passage, quoted by the same author: ' Nam in ipsis reipublicæ nostræ rudimentis, cum aliqua adhuc barbaries Scotiam occupasset, quosdam duces, *thanos*, vernacula lingua vocabant; illustri familia ortos delegerunt, quibus se suamque familiam regendam committebant.'—And Buchanan: ' Superioribus sæculis, præter *thanos*, hoc est, præfectos regionum, sive monarchas, &c. nullum honoris nomen equestri ordine altius.'

Gurdon, in his History of court-baron and court-leet, gives a very copious account of the origin and dignity of the English *thane*. I shall quote his definition of the word, and something relating to the *thane*'s power and jurisdiction; but must refer the reader to the book itself for farther information:

' The Saxon word *thane*, or *thegne*, implies *minister*, or *servant*; one who was an honorary servant to the king in the field and in council, not a servant under absolute command, but obliged, by fœderal union, to serve the king in war and council, of one and the other's property.' Gurdon's parliaments, &c. p. 537.

' The *thane* had the same jurisdiction in his soke, or manor, as the king had in his great signiory; but neither of them were absolute. The king, in the great signiory, determined by and with the advice of his *thanes*, as original sharers

with

with the king in the conquered lands; and the *thane*, in the court of his foke, or little figniory, determined all differences between his men in their civil rights, and also punifhed criminals, with the advice and confent of his freemen. Life and death were at firft within the jurifdiction of the *thane*'s hall-mote.' Ibidem.

To pafs by unnoticed the obfervations of the accomplifhed Mrs. Montague, on Macbeth, would be uncandid and unjuft. Her reflections are the product of mature and folid judgment, conveyed in language at once forcible and elegant.

Julius Cæsar.

CHAP. XXIX.

Shakspeare's predilection for Brutus.—His character of Cæsar.—Cæsar's weakness.—The reception of Julius Cæsar when originally acted.—Leonard Diggs.—Hart and Mohun, their excellence in Brutus and Cassius.—Rymer's opinion of their skill.—Lord Rochester's character of Mohun.—Duke of Buckingham's Cæsar and Brutus.—Voltaire's Mort de César.—Abbé de Fontaines.—Hill's Roman Revenge.—Quotation from it.—Shakspeare unjustly criticised.—Roman and English mechanics alike.—A muleteer made a tribune of Rome.—Honour in one hand and death in the other.—Cassius's character.—Winstone, Quin, Mills, Milward, and W. Mills.—Julius Cæsar not acted under Garrick's management.—Why.—C. Ligarius.—Bowman.—Quin jealous of his applause.—Roman actors.—Their indefatigable application.—Nero, an actor.—His fear of an audience.—Æsopus and Roscius—The public spirit of Æsopus—Players must obey audiences.—The Roman ear delicate.—Æsopus obliged to observe the powers of his voice. Roman actors limited to particular parts.—Æsopus.—Moliere and Colley Cibber.—Riches of a Roman actor.—Roscius, a rival of Cicero in gesticulation.—A great teacher of acting.—Roman slaves.—Cicero's character of Roscius.

THE tragedy of Julius Cæsar seems to have been written by Shakspeare with a design to introduce his favourite character of Brutus. The author, who had carried the notions of indefeasible right, of passive obedience, and non resistance, in many parts of his works, as far as any of the politicians and divines of his time, in this play, seems to have adopted more liberal principles of government, and to have indulged sentiments purely democratical. As he drew his knowledge of Roman characters from Plutarch, it is surprizing he should have drawn so deficient a portrait of Cæsar. Little of it has he preserved except his undaunted courage and attractive urbanity. He has likewise not forgotten his contempt of dreams, omens, forebodings, and every species of superstition. But the poet has made him, what he never was, an ostentatious boaster, and a violent rejector of the petitions addressed to him. But perhaps Cæsar was to be lessened in order to aggrandize Brutus.

It must however be said, in excuse of our great dramatist, that he has confined himself to that period of time, immediately preceding the death of the dictator. His original, Plutarch, relates that his conduct then was of a different complexion from what it had formerly been. Success seems to have rendered Cæsar forgetful of his situation; and his behaviour to the senate, in not rising up to salute them when they approached him, was justly reprehensible. But his passion for the kingly title, so odious to his countrymen, was a glaring proof of his imbecility; since he possessed all the power of royalty under a title less obnoxious to censure, that of Dictator. The preserving the names of old titles, and offices, is the least compliment, that he, who seizes the supreme power, can pay to the manes of departed liberty; and this artful behaviour has often established more firmly a new system of government raised upon the ruins of the old. Though Shakspeare has put into the mouth of Cæsar more than usual severity of expression in rejecting the petition and intreaties of Metellus Cimber in behalf of his brother, yet there is sufficient ground in Plutarch to suppose, that the persisting clamours of the conspirators drew from him an answer of more than usual asperity. But indeed Plutarch himself is accused, by his last translators, of giving a very imperfect draft of Cæsar's character.

Notwithstanding Nat. Lee, in his dedication of his Junius Brutus, has asserted that the Brutus of our author could, with much ado, beat himself into the heads of a blockish age: we have authority, from two copies of verses written by Leonard Diggs, prefixed to the plays and the sonnets of Shakspeare, that the audience were in raptures with the play of Julius Cæsar, and more especially with the admired scene, in Act IV. between Brutus and Cassius:

———Till I hear a scene more nobly take
Than when *the half-sword playing Romans spake*.

     Works of Shakspeare, 1623.

So I have seen, when Cæsar would appear,
And on the stage at half-sword parley were
Brutus and Cassius! *O! how the audience
Were ravish'd! with what wonder went they hence!*

     Shakspeare's sonnets, 1640.

Dryden himself confesses he was fired with this noble scene, and ashamed of his own want of genius to rival Shakspeare. But Brutus could be no favourite in the reign of Charles II. when government was a factious conspiracy against the rights of the people, and every friend of liberty was branded as a fomenter of sedition. However, Julius Cæsar amongst the few plays of our great poet which were revived soon after the Restoration, was one selected from the royal list given the players of the King's Theatre in Drury-Lane, by Hart and Mohun, in which they greatly signalized themselves, and especially Mohun, who, for his excellent performance of Cassius is commended by Downs the stage historian, and still to his greater honour, applauded by Lord Rochester. That we have no memoirs or relations but what can be gathered from Downs, and some traditional scraps and slight notices of poets and critics of these two great actors, is to be lamented. Their rank in life, having both been honoured with commands in the army, placed them above their fellows. Rymer, the celebrated critic and historiographer, has applauded them highly for their wonderful power of fixing the attention of the audience, and speaking to them as much by action as utterance. Mohun was particularly remarkable for the dignity of his deportment and graceful manner of treading the stage. The Earl of Rochester reproaches the comedians of the Duke of York's company for their vain attempts to ape his excellences, and ridiculing his defects, the consequences of age and infirmity.

Yet

Yet these are they who durst expose the age
Of the great wonder of the English stage,
Whom nature seem'd to form for your delight,
And bade him speak, as she bade Shakspeare write:
These blades indeed are cripples in their art,
Mimic the foot, but not the speaking part;
Let them the Traitor or Volpone try:
———————————Could they———
Rage like Cethegus, or like Cassius die?

    Sheffield Duke of Buckingham, observing there was a double plot in this play, sat down to form two tragedies out of one, Julius Cæsar, and the death of Marcus Brutus. Whether they are strictly conformable to the rules of the drama, and observe the unities, I have not so critically examined them as to determine, but he seems to have taken great pains to extinguish the noble fire of the original. The style, except where Shakspeare is preserved, is correctly cold and regularly dull, uninformed by the spirit of genius to give life to the whole mass. His grace has introduced upon the stage what our poet has only related, Cæsar's refusal of the crown offered to him by Mark Antony at the Lupercal games. The account of this transaction, by Casca in the original, is humourously circumstantial, but the exhibition of it on the stage, in the new Julius Cæsar, is tedious and prosaic. The reader may judge from a short specimen of it.

Antony presenting Julius Cæsar with the crown.

Hail! mighty man, thou godlike Cæsar, hail!
Stoop to our wishes, and vouchsafe to wear
This crown, presented thee by all mankind:
Shine on us like the sun in his full lustre,
Adorn us with your power, and make us proud
Of being subjects to so great a king.

                                                CÆSAR.

CÆSAR.

I am not call'd your king, but your dictator,
A name I hope that bears as great a sound,
Therefore, I both refuse and slight the crown,
Which can add nothing to my power or Rome's:
  [*Cæsar puts back the crown, and the people shout.*
I am glad, my friends, you are so easily pleas'd
With my refusing what I think below me, &c.

The whole scene is written in the same frigid manner; the reader will find that Buckingham is seldom warmed with the bright blaze of the original, which, like the vestal virgin, he had taken in his custody to preserve and cherish.

La Mort de César of Voltaire is one of the least valuable of all this great writer's dramatic pieces. From a hatred, I suppose, of republican freedom, he has adopted the story of Brutus being Cæsar's son by Servilia, the sister of Cato. But the improbability of this story is evident from Cæsar's being little more than fourteen years of age when Brutus was born. Voltaire's tragedy is in three acts; without women, and consequently free from love: how he could suppose a play, deficient in such essentials, could please so gay a nation as the French, is not very easy to imagine. I do not remember that the Greeks, whom the French profess to follow, have any tragedy without females, except the Philoctetes of Sophocles. The Abbé de Fontaines, a mercenary writer, in a periodical work of which he had the direction, attacked with acrimony La Mort de César: Voltaire was alarmed, but found an infallible method of softening this Cerberus; for the abbé some time after pretended that he had been unhappily misled, by the errors of the press, to censure

sure a play of such uncommon merit; for such, says he, I found it, after perusing a true copy of the original.

Aaron Hill formed his Roman Revenge upon Voltaire's Death of Cæsar.—But he much enlarged and improved the plan, not only by the addition of two characters, Calphurnia and Portia, but with a number of others, besides great variety of action. Hill seems to have idolized the character of Cæsar, whom he drew in the most amiable colours, representing him to be the worthiest and most amiable of men. The same fondness for monarchical principles, which misled Voltaire to make Brutus the son of Cæsar, infected Hill, who has adopted the same idle tale; the father breaks the secret to the son, who receives it with surprise and dread, but, after much struggling between nature and principle, and a long suspence between the love of liberty and the horror of destroying a parent, he is yet impelled, by the artful contrivance of the conspirators and his own enthusiastic notions of Rome and liberty, to become an associate in Cæsar's murder. This play, though strongly recommended and approved by Lord Bolingbroke and Mr. Pope, did not please the managers or actors. Neither Quin nor Garrick could be prevailed upon to act this demi-god, Cæsar. And indeed, although there are many admirable sentiments and some affecting scenes in the Roman Revenge, it is so stiffened with epithet, bespangled with antithesis, and decorated with pointed thought, all which he has marked in Italic letters, that the players would have found it very difficult to utter the lines trippingly, as Shakspeare says, from the tongue; the audience would not have relished a

Brutus

Brutus so differently drawn from that of their favourite Shakspeare; neither would they have borne with a patriot who could lift the murdering sword against his own father. The reader will judge of the style from a short specimen taken from a scene, where the father and son plead in behalf of their different forms of government.

CÆSAR.

Rome's senate, rich and proud, oppress'd her people:
Her people, poor and head-strong, spurn'd their yoke:
Hence rose the new necessity, thou know'st not,
Of some unformal self-supporting *sword*,
To cut sedition boldly *to the root*,
And rectify the crooked growth of empire:
This done, *degen'rate* Rome grows fit for liberty:
Make it thy future gift and therefore reign.
Now 'tis sedition's cloak, her trumpet's *call.*

BRUTUS.

———————Teach the senate
These fond defects, and shape their wish'd redress:
Their's is the right to think for *council'd Rome.*
Cæsar a king! were all his virtues stars,
Rome's rights invading makes his virtues crimes.
Cæsar's a citizen, protecting law,
Mix'd with the people, reigns the people's god.

Act I.   Scene I.

Flavius, Marcellus, and other Commoners.

Shakspeare is accused of giving the manners of London to the inhabitants of any other part of the globe to which he transports his spectators: what! says the critic, compare the Roman citizens to an English mob, by giving them the rude

rude behaviour of our artisans? Had not then the Romans carpenters, bricklayers, and shoemakers, as well as ourselves? The Roman populace were not a whit more polished than our own. It is natural for every mechanic to talk in the language of his own trade, like the honest cobler in this scene, who ingenuously tells the tribunes, he leads the people up and down the streets of Rome to wear out their shoes, that he may have more work. I have seen old Ben Jonson, the player, personate this little part with great humour.

These gentlemen, who think the great masters of the world were too polite and well-bred to be represented like our English mechanics, should read some of Cicero's epistles, and more especially his oration in defence of Publius Sextius against Clodius: there they will find more wickedness, outrage, and mischief, perpetrated by Clodius's mob, than he ever heard was committed by an English rabble. He will be convinced, too, that the Romans were as vulgar and boisterous, and much more corrupt, and selfish, than our own people. A muleteer was, by an odd vicissitude of fortune, advanced to the dignity of a Roman tribune; this fellow was employed by Clodius, as a fit agent, to promote his riot; but his own people having, as they imagined, killed a tribune of the opposite party, Clodius determined to make the matter even by sacrificing the life of the muleteer; but he, apprehending the danger, had recourse to his old habit of muledriving, and, with a basket on his head, escaped the intended assassination.

BRUTUS.

BRUTUS.

> Set honour in one eye and death in the other,
> And I will look on *both indifferently* ———
> For let the Gods so speed me as I love
> The name of honour more than I fear death.

Dr. Warburton, instead of *both indifferently*, reads *death indifferently*. Dr. Johnson supports with great plausibility the other reading. *Indifferently*, I think, in this place, means, I will consider both with *coolness* and *impartiality*. Buckingham has, in my opinion, rather mangled than improved the sense of the author in this place:

> Set virtue in one eye, and let grim death
> Shake his unheeded dart, I'll still be fix'd:
> For may the gods so help me, as for honour
> I look indifferently on life and death.

Quin, I remember, spoke the word in dispute as Warburton altered it.

CASCA.

> You pull'd me by the cloak, would you speak with me?

During the scene in which Casca relates the behaviour of Cæsar in the lupercal games, where Antony offers him the crown, the character of the relator is supported with great humour. In act II. he unexpectedly appears a different man: however the author has justified this conduct from the mouth of Cassius, who tells us, that his dogged manner was not his own, but assumed. The poet, having no business for Casca after the murder of Cæsar, has dropt him in act III. but the players, finding their company not numerous enough to supply all the characters of this play,

many

many years since enlarged Casca, by adding to his part what belongs to Titinius. Julius Cæsar was one of the three plays acted by the desire of the prime nobility in Queen Anne's time, with the united strength of the then two companies. Casca, if I remember right, was acted by a principal comedian. Above five and forty years since, Winstone was selected for that character, when Quin acted Brutus, and the elder Mills Cassius, Milward M. Antony, and W. Mills Julius Cæsar. The assumed doggedness and sourness of Casca sat well upon Winstone. The four principal parts have not since that time been equally presented. Mr. Garrick, pleased with the spirit and fire of Cassius, once determined to have tried his skill in that part; but, whether he thought he should only swell the consequence of his competitor Quin in Brutus, or from what other cause, I know not, he relinquished his intention: nor was this excellent play revived during his management of the stage, though I am of opinion he wanted not actors of merit to do considerable justice to the play.

Scene VI.

Casca and Cicero.

So important a man as Cicero should not have been introduced in a scene of so little signification as the relation of a prodigy. The players have very judiciously left it out in the representation.

Act II. Scene I.

BRUTUS.

————O! Conspiracy————by day
Where wilt thou find a cavern deep enough
To mask thy monstrous visage? seek none, Conspiracy!
Hide it in smiles and affability.————

Sentiments like these are not unfrequent in Shakspeare: Brutus repeats the same once or twice in this very scene. So, when Macbeth has determined to murder his royal master, he resolves to hide his dark intention by dissembled courtesy and over-acted show of duty.

————Away, and mock the time with fairest show;
False face must hide what the false heart doth know.
Macbeth, Act 2d.

CAIUS LIGARIUS [to BRUTUS]

———————— Set on your foot,
And, with a heart new fir'd, I'll follow you
To do I know not what, but it sufficeth
That Brutus leads me on.

Bowman, who had acted this part of Ligarius more than fifty years, was advanced above the age of fourscore when I saw him perform it; he assumed great vigour and a truly Roman spirit. The applause which he obtained, and justly merited, was not relished by Quin, who neglected to pay that attention to the character which he ought. This is a fault which I have observed in some principal actors, who have treated their inferiors of the stage with disregard, because they were below them in rank as comedians, though the parts they acted demanded observance to be paid

paid them, at least before the public, to support that stage-deception, without which a play loses its effect.

BRUTUS.

Let not our looks put on our purposes;
But bear it, as our Roman actors do,
With untir'd spirits and formal constancy.

Whether Shakspeare intended in these lines to celebrate the persevering labour and indefatigable spirit of the actor in general, or the Roman actor in particular, is perhaps doubtful. That the skill of the latter was put to a much severer trial than that of a modern comedian cannot well be denied. It is much easier to please, I should imagine, sixteen or seventeen hundred persons, shut up in a small building, than sixty or seventy thousand spectators who behold a play from a spacious amphitheatre. But to drop this argument, which is perhaps more specious than solid, we have good authority to say that the Roman actors were uncommonly solicitous to please their judges, and extremely fearful of incurring their displeasure. Nero, when he acted a part on the stage, felt the greatest anxiety lest he should be subject to the displeasure of the spectators.

Suetonius, in the life of this emperor, relates, that, during the time of the representation, he observed the laws of the theatre so punctually, that he never ventured to spit, nor to wipe off the sweat from his forehead except with his elbow. As he was once acting in a tragedy he let his staff, or truncheon, fall out of his hand; and, though he recovered it immediately, his terror and affright were so great, lest he should be hissed off the stage, that he could not compose himself, till one of the players swore no notice was taken of it, amidst the noise and acclamations of the people.

The very dress of the Roman actor was, from the richness of habit and variety of ornament, in the characters of heroes and demi-gods, a perfect burthen to the wearer. To appear like Hercules, he must be stuffed in the body and raised upon elevated buskins. The *niti cothurno* of Horace has its literal, as well as metaphorical, meaning; to walk gracefully upon such supporters must have required great practice and much art. The masque, too, covered the head and shoulders, and was adorned with large plumage and other decorations.

Cicero has given honourable testimony of the two celebrated Roman actors, Æsopus and Roscius, men whom he ranked in the number of his friends, and styled his *Deliciæ*. To the former, indeed, he was indebted for the foundation of his eloquence; by his lessons he attained to that consummate art in speaking, which rendered him the first orator of his time.* But Æsopus was not more admired for his skill in his profession, than for the love he bore his country, and for inviolable attachment to his friend.

During Cicero's exile, and at a time when his friends had procured a decree of the senate for his recal from banishment, Æsopus, says Cicero, who performed the same good part in public which he did upon the stage, was acting the part of Telamon, who was banished from his country, in one of Accius's

---

* Melmoth's Epistles of Cicero, vol. I. p. 119. The Grecian actors were still more accomplished than the Romans. Histriones Græci plerumque erant homines docti, et ingenui oratores et poetæ, et in artibus aliis spectabiles. G. I. Vossius, Inst. Poetic.

us's plays. By the particular emphasis of his voice, and a change of a word or two in some of the lines, he dextrously contrived to turn the thoughts of the audience upon Cicero——*What, he! who always stood up for the republic!—Who in doubtful times spared neither life nor fortune!—The firmest friend in the most imminent danger!—Of such parts and talents!—O father!—I saw his house and rich furniture all in flames!*—By peculiar address the actor so managed, that at the end of every sentence the applauses were incessant: and, in another tragedy of the same author, called Brutus,† when, instead of *Brutus*, Æsopus pronounced *Tullius*, who established the liberty of his citizens, the people were so affected, they called for it again a thousand times.

And here I cannot help observing, that the player, as the servant and creature of the public, ought not to refuse repeating any line or sentence that he has once pronounced on the stage, when demanded by the spectators. Much has been said, in a late stage-history ‡, of the folly of an audience, in exacting the reiteration of some particular lines in the tragedy of Mahomet acted on the Dublin theatre some years since, and which were applied to the politics of the times. If there be really any absurdity in the case, it lies at the door of those who can best answer it, the people assembled in the theatre. To hazard the displeasure of those, who have the power to inforce their orders, is equally impolitic and dangerous; as the manager of the Dublin theatre found it, to his great damage.

Notwith-

---

† Cicero pro P. Sextio.—Middleton's life of Cicero, vol. I.
‡ Victor's History of the Stage.

Notwithstanding the highest estimation in which Æsopus was held with the public, so nice and delicate was the Roman ear, that he durst not venture to exhibit with the smallest defect in his power of utterance or the least approach to hoarseness. If the modulation of his voice was disturbed by a cold, or any accidental impediment, they immediately reproved him by evident marks of their displeasure. The nursing of the voice was attended with particular solicitude by the Roman actors, † and certain regulations were formed to manage its various inflections. Besides this, the poet gave the actor certain rules in writing, like notes in music, by which the tones of his voice, in uttering either sentiment or passion, were to be governed. The actors were circumscribed too within the limits of their particular talents and abilities: those, whose voices could reach the extent of passion, acted parts of loud vehemence; those, who excelled chiefly in action and deportment, were directed to suitable characters. Æsopus, says Cicero, did not often try the difficult part of Ajax. §

This great actor, several years after he had quitted the stage, in a very advanced time of life, was called upon to honour the opening of Pompey's theatre with his performance; but unhappily he only exposed his imbecility, and was dismissed with pity. Æsopus, attempting to pronounce a solemn oath, his voice failed him, and he could not utter distinctly the words *Si sciens fallo.* Moliere, in spite of a decaying constitution and a nervous habitual cough, would, in contradiction to the remonstrances of his

† Cicero de Oratore.   § Cicero de Officiis.

his friends, persist to act, as this amiable man declared, for the good of his people. In his last play of the Hypochondriac he was seized with a convulsion, in pronouncing the word *juro*, and died a few days after.——About the time Mr. Garrick charmed the public with Shakspeare's character of Richard III. Colley Cibber in his old age was impelled by his vanity to resume the part, to which, notwithstanding all that he and his friends have said about his performance of it, he was by no means equal; for his cracked pipe could not give force to the animated scenes of the two last acts of Richard III. Cibber's success was little better than that of Æsopus; he was dismissed indeed, like the Roman actor, with no marks of displeasure; but mere sufferance, in such a situation is rather an humiliating circumstance. Victor, who saw him when the play was over, told me that Colley confessed he never longed so much for any thing as the dying scene of Richard. Macklin indeed acted the same part at seventy-five with as strong a voice as he was master of at forty five; but where shall we find two Macklins?

Æsopus died immensely rich; Melmoth estimates his property at 200000l. I should imagine it to be twice as much; for if he could give a feast, as we are informed he did, at which one dish alone cost him near 4900l. what must be the amount of the whole?

But the abilities of Roscius seem to have exceeded those of his friend Æsopus. So well did he understand the various powers of action, that he contested with Cicero to express as perfectly by gesture as the orator could by elocution. His character is so well known, that I shall dwell the less upon it.

Notwithstanding his perverse or squinting eyes, the Romans were better pleased with him when he played without a mask than with one * He was a great teacher in the art of acting, and acquired great riches by it. For, of all the Roman slaves, those, who were capable of being taught to act, brought their masters the largest profit.‡ Slaves who could read were sold, according to Dr. Arbuthnot, at 807*l*. 5*s*. 10*d*. We may guess from thence the value of the others. Roscius was so hard to please, that he declared, he never could find a pupil whom he entirely approved; not but that he had the instruction of many youths of very great abilities; but his consummate knowledge could discover defects unperceived by every body else. When he was advanced to old age, he changed his mode of recitation; he spoke not with the same rapidity as formerly; his tones were then more soft and deliberate, and the music was accommodated to the voice. In his Oration for Archias, the poet, Cicero embraces an opportunity to pay respect to the memory of Roscius. 'Where amongst us,' says the Orator, 'is the mind so barbarous, where is the heart so unfeeling, as to be unaffected with the death of Roscius?' He died indeed in a very advanced age, but he was a man who by his art and elegance seemed to challenge immortality to his person. Q. Catulus pronounced this man to be more beautiful than the rising sun, notwithstanding his squinting eyes and his distorted looks.

Consti-

---

* Cicero.   ‡ Plinii Nat. Hist. lib. x.

Constiteram, exorientem Auroram forte salutans,
  Cum subito a læva Roscius exoritur.
Pace mihi liceat, cœlestes, dicere vestra,
  Mortalis visu'it pulchrior esse Deo.

   Huic, Deo pulchrior.———At erat, sicut hodie est, perver-
sissimis oculis.

   Q. Catulus apud Ciceronem de Nat. Deorum.

CHAP.

CHAP. XXX.

Cæsar's urbanity.—Question of Cæsar's death.—The oppressive spirit of the senate.—Aristocracy and oligarchy.—Tiberius and Caius Gracchus.—Number of Roman citizens when Cæsar was murdered.—Panem et circenses.—Cæsar's abilities.—His clemency.—Perfidy of conspirators.—Romans disqualified to entertain freedom.—Number of slaves in Rome.—Rich furniture and buildings of the Romans.—Luxury of the Romans.—Price of a mullus.—Son of Æsopus.—His profuseness.—The pleasure of seeing fish expire.—Difficulty in representing the assassination of Cæsar.—Actors of Julius Cæsar.—Goodman, Colley Cibber, and the Dutchess of Cleveland.—Alexander the great.—Goodman a highwayman.—Antony's servant, and Brutus.—Wilks's action.—Speech of Antony.—Antony well paid for his oratory.—Isocrates and Demosthenes.—Defects of Wilks.—Barry's powers.—Milward's excellences.—The word villain.—Baite and bay.—Brutus and Cassius.—Booth and Quin.—If that thou be'st a Roman explained.—Quin.—Abbé le Blanc and David Garrick.—Scene between Amintor and Melantius.—Hector and Troilus.—Dorax and Sebastian.—Agamemnon and Menelaus.—The conclusion.

Act II. Scene II.

Cæsar, Brutus, C. Ligarius, Antony, &c.

CÆSAR.

———————— Caius Ligarius,
Cæsar was ne'er so much your enemy
As that same ague which hath made you lean.

THERE is scarce any part of Cæsar's character so well understood by Shakspeare, as the great urbanity of his manners, and the ease and affability of his conversation. If Cæsar was the greatest soldier, he seems likewise to have been the best-bred man of all antiquity. In this short scene his address varies with the character of the person to whom he speaks. The compliment he pays to Caius Ligarius is a happy mixture of politeness and humanity.

Act III. The senate.

The assassination of Cæsar.

CÆSAR.

Et tu, Brute!

As Decimus Brutus was a great favourite of Cæsar, it is perhaps doubtful, whether *Et tu, Brute!* was addressed to him or Marcus Brutus; however it is universally understood to have been spoken to the latter.

CINNA.

Liberty! freedom!——tyranny is dead!

The question of Cæsar's death has long been agitated, between the abettors of absolute monarchy, and the friends of a republican form of government. The dispute has been managed with as much eagerness, as if their different state-establishments were highly interested in the justification or condemnation of the act. Perhaps, after all, the decision of the dispute may not affect the principles of either party.

The proper question is, whether the state of Rome gained or lost by Cæsar's murder, not whether Cæsar deserved to be put to death. What sort of liberty did the assassins propose to establish after they had killed him? The democratical power of the Republic, which I will presume to say was the most essential to the welfare of the people, had long since been extinguished, or at least so diminished, that its efficacy was dwindled to almost nothing. The senate had seized into their hands the whole power of the state; the people enjoyed no more than that small pittance of freedom which their lords and masters were willing to allow them. But the conscript fathers themselves were controuled and kept in awe by a small number of their own members, who, from time to time, seized upon all offices and honours of the state, and distributed them amongst their friends and followers. Thus was the aristocracy melted down into an oligarchy.

Since the murder of their two great tribunes, Tiberius and Caius Gracchus, the Romans had enjoyed nothing but the shadow of liberty. These

These men lost their lives in a generous attempt to rescue the poor from the oppression of the rich. After their deaths, the power of the tribune, an office created to protect the rights and privileges of the plebeians, became, by the chicanery and injustice of the senate, an engine of power to enslave and impoverish the people. The domination of Sylla completed the destruction of the tribunitian authority. He not only deprived them of their rights of legislation, but he passed a decree, by which every man who had served that office was rendered incapable of occupying any other. The triumvirate of Pompey, Cæsar, and Crassus, succeeded in a very short space of time to the usurped power of Sylla; and, during the interval between that and the dictatorship of Cæsar, hired mobs, riots, and tumults, formed to support the illegal pretensions of the several candidates for the offices of the state continually alarmed and disturbed the peace of the city. The provinces were infamously oppressed by the proconsuls. Those, whom we call English nabobs, are not said to be more solicitous to accumulate immense riches, by plundering whole principalities, and robbing the princes of the East, than these Roman governors were eager to pillage the nations over whom they were sent to preside. They deprived them of every thing that was valuable, in money and plate, pictures, jewels, pearls, statues, or any thing esteemed an object of taste or avarice. The plebeians were become the willing slaves of the patricians, who, to gain their votes and interest, fed them with largesses, and diverted them with shows at an exorbitant expence. The number of Roman citizens, who were proprietors of land when Cæsar was put to death, did not, by computation, amount to more than two thousand.* And this is an evident proof of the oppression and injustice of the senate, and the profligacy and corruption of all orders in the state. Give us honours, titles, and emoluments, said the great to the populace, and in return, we will give you money and shows. *Panem et circenses* was even then all that the free citizens of Rome desired. And were these the men for whom the life of Cæsar was to be sacrificed? We are told, indeed, that the best and wisest of the Romans approved of the murder of Cæsar. It is strange that even experience should not have convinced these Romans that liberty could not be a blessing to a mob of slaves. Cicero, one of the wisest men in Rome, was persecuted and exposed to banishment for saving his country from the desperate conspiracy of Catiline; nor would he, perhaps, have been freed from exile, if the two great kings of Rome, Pompey and Cæsar, had not been disgusted with their infamous tool Clodius.

In this distracted state of Rome, at the close of the civil war, the only man, capable to establish some regular form of government, was Julius Cæsar. His abilities in the cabinet were as solid as his actions in the field were splendid. The qualities of his mind were noble, generous, and humane; of all the Romans, who had drawn the sword against their countrymen, he was acknowledged to have been the most merciful.

It is impossible to justify the conspirators upon any reasonable principle: they had been obliged as far as men could be obliged; they had been taken

* Gibbon's decline of the Roman Empire. Vol. III.

taken in arms fighting againſt Cæſar, for Pompey, not for the republic: they were reſtored to their country and to the enjoyment of the honours of the ſtate; ſeveral of them had received employments from the hands of Cæſar. Antony's reproach in act V. of the play, that, when they were preparing their daggers for his throat, they cried, *all hail, Cæſar!* was juſt. For, in the daily intercourſe of friendſhip and reciprocation of mutual offices, to plot a man's death is the groſſeſt violation of thoſe ſocial bands which unite men together, that can poſſibly be deviſed. We may, with all the appearance of truth, conclude, that the conſpirators hated all tyranny but their own; ariſtocracy was the idol for which they fought and died; and that is, of all forms of government, the beſt ſuited to men of intolerant principles, and the moſt oppreſſive to the people. God forbid that England ſhould be ever governed by a houſe of lords! and this I do not ſay from a want of due reverence to that auguſt aſſembly.

Many cauſes concurred to render the people of Rome diſqualified to receive that liberty which Brutus and the conſpirators pretended to offer them. They no more reſembled the Romans who lived during the free days of the Republic than the Ægyphan mob, in Dryden's play of Cleomenes King of Sparta, were like the Greeks, who endeavoured to inſpire them with a ſenſe of liberty; a word, ſays Dryden, which they pronounced ſo feebly, that they ſeemed afraid of its being heard. Rome was at that time a mart of ſlaves and ſlavery; we cannot ſuppoſe that the precincts of Rome contained leſs than 500000 ſlaves. Many of the great men had no leſs than 20000

20000 in their retinue, most of them for pomp and ostentation. Luxury of all kinds was carried to excess. The great contention was, who should have the most magnificent houses in Rome, and villas out of it, with the richest and most costly furniture. They cased their houses with marble, and their doors were plated with gold. They had tables of gold and precious stones, and drinking-cups estimated at 2 or 3000*l*. Julius Cæsar lay on a golden bed with a purple covering. They had candlesticks estimated at the salary of a tribune, 403*l.* 12*s.* 11*d.* their passion for plate, jewels, and all kind of precious stones, was insatiable. Julius Cæsar presented Servilia, Brutus's mother, with a pearl worth 48437*l.* 10*s.* The luxury of the table went in the same pace with all the rest; a Roman of those times would have fought more lustily for a mullus, a fish not weighing above two pounds, and supposed to be the same as our surmullet, than for the cause of liberty: they rose in price from 30*l.* to 60*l.* What shall we think of the humanity of a Roman senator who fed his lampreys with the flesh of his condemned slaves? and of a supper given to two great men by a friend, which cost him 1614*l.* 11*s.* 8*d.* * One young gentleman, the son of a player, Æsopus, treated his guests with costly pearl; a pearl for every guest made into pearl-cordial. I shall mention another species of luxury which is yet unknown to a modern table, though perhaps a nabob of taste may some time hence think of introducing it as an improvement fit for his savoir-vivre company. The Romans weighed their fishes at table, and took a pleasure in beholding

---

* An entertainment, without any previous notice, given by Lucullus to Pompey and Cicero. Arbuthnot on Coins.

holding them expire. The death of a mullus, with the variety and change of colours in its laſt moments, ſays Dr. Arbuthnot from Pliny, was reckoned one of the moſt entertaining ſpectacles in the world. And now, I hope, we ſhall hear no more of the wiſeſt and beſt men among the Romans approving the aſſaſſination of Julius Cæſar.

From the great number of perſons on the ſtage, during the repreſentation of Cæſar's murder, much difficulty in the action may ariſe, unleſs great accuracy is obſerved in the direction of thoſe who are employed. The ſeveral conſpirators, preſſing with eagerneſs to have a ſhare in ſtabbing the victim, muſt be ſo regulated as to prevent confuſion. Cæſar's anxiety to fall with decency, by covering his body with his mantle, ſhould be in the actor's memory; nor ſhould the manager forget to have a figure of a ſtatue, ſuppoſed to reſemble that of Pompey; the poet expreſsly mentions Cæſar's falling at his great rival's feet, and ſprinkling his ſtatue with his blood.

Who acted the part of Julius Cæſar originally is not known, nor is it a matter of importance. But ſoon after the junction of the King's and Duke of York's company, about the year 1682, this tragedy was in all its parts ſo acted as it never had been perhaps before, and certainly has not ſince: Betterton Brutus, Smith Caſſius, Mark Antony by Kynaſton, and Julius Cæſar by Goodman. Griffin, Mountfort, Williams, Gillow, Jevon, Underhill, and Leigh, all very eminent actors, thought it no diminution of their conſequence to play the inferior parts.

Goodman was a very handsome gay fellow, as well as a very confiderable performer on the ftage. But Goodman's paffions were ftrong and his appetites larger than his very moderate income of about 30 or 40 fhillings per week could fatisfy. And, to procure fuch pleafures as he moft delighted in, he was reduced, as Colley Cibber fays, to try his fortune on the highway. Whether it was after the road-adventure, or before, that the Dutchefs of Cleveland threw her amorous glances on Goodman is not clear from ftage-hiftory. But I fhould rather think that it happened afterwards that he fell into the dutchefs's good graces. For Goodman, long before his death, was fo happy in his finances, that he acted only occafionally, perhaps when his noble miftrefs wifhed to fee him in a principal character; for Goodman ufed to fay, *he would never act Alexander the Great, but when he was certain that his dutchefs would be in the boxes to fee him perform.* Cibber relates, with nonchalance, that Goodman entered into a plot to affaffinate King William, he fuppofes from gratitude to James II. who had pardoned his robbery on the highway.

Julius Cæfar was, in the opinion of the elder Mills, the part in tragedy which his fon William acted with moft propriety. I remember to have feen him perform it; and though he was in general a fnip-fnap fpeaker, a manner which Mr. Garrick very happily mimicked in the Rehearfal, when fpeaking before Mills himfelf, yet in Cæfar he gave fuch an idea of the part as Shakfpeare intended.

Scene

Scene continues.

ANTONY's SERVANT.

So fays my mafter Antony.

BRUTUS.

Thy mafter is a wife and valiant Roman,
I never thought him worfe.

That Antony was valiant, cannot be denied: his beft praife is, that he was a good foldier; but that he was wife, which comprehends moral virtue, or it means nothing, is a fentiment unworthy the mouth of Brutus. Nor fhould our author have drawn his favourite either fo ignorant a judge, or fo grofs a flatterer of the moft abandoned follower of Cæfar's fortunes.

MARK ANTONY.

O mighty Cæfar, art thou fallen fo low!

Wilks, who above fifty years fince acted Mark Antony, as foon as he entered the ftage, without taking any notice of the confpirators, walked fwiftly up to the dead body of Cæfar and knelt down; he paufed fome time before he fpoke; and, after furveying the corpfe with manifeft tokens of the deepeft forrow, he addreffed it in a moft affecting and pathetic manner. A graceful dignity accompanied the action and deportment of this actor.

IDEM.

I do befeech you, if you bear me hard.

That is, *if you owe me any ill will.*

This is a frequent mode of expression with Shakspeare, and occurs no less than three times in acts II. and III. of this play.

IDEM.

Friends! Romans! countrymen!

It has not, I believe, been hitherto observed by any of the commentators, that this admirable piece of oratory, so happily divided into exordium, narration, and peroration, is the sole product of our author's genius, unassisted by his conductor, Plutarch. The only hint, which he has borrowed from that writer, is Antony's shewing the dead body of Cæsar to the populace: it is composed of such topics as were most conducive to the desired effect. The artful pauses and interruptions serve to increase the skill and power of the speaker, and to rouse, astonish, and inflame, the minds of the auditors. The Duke of Buckingham has very prudently preserved almost the whole of Antony's oration as the author wrote it, though he has presumed to alter every other scene in the play.

No orator ever met with so ample a reward for a single oration as Antony did for this funeral harangue over the body of Cæsar. The Grecian orators had large sums for their speeches. Isocrates received from Nicocles King of Cyprus, for one oration, no less a sum than 3875*l*. and Demosthenes obtained from Harpalus 4000*l*. for one day's silence. The sum Antony paid for Cicero's head, an article that may well come into the account of eloquence, was 8072*l*. 18*s*. 4*d*. being ten times more than was offered for any other pro-

proscribed person. † The Roman orators had frequently the causes of kings, provinces, and cities, to plead, and were paid according to the riches and generosity of the employers. But Antony took care to be his own pay-master. He was in-debted, March 15, the day on which Cæsar was murdered, to the amount of 322916*l*. 13*s*. 4*d*. which immense sum, by the fraudulent management of Cæsar's papers, he discharged before the first of April following. *

The action of Wilks in Antony, from the beginning to the end of the oration, was critically adapted to produce the intended consequences of the speaker. His address through the whole was easy and elegant; but his voice wanted that fulness and variety, requisite to impress the sentiments and pathos with which the speech abounds: besides, Wilks was apt to strike the syllables too forcibly as well as uniformly. Mr. Barry's fine person and pleasing manner were well adapted to Mark Antony, but his utterance in recitation of sentiment was not sufficiently sonorous, nor his voice flexible enough, to express the full meaning of the author in the opening of the address. When roused by passion, Barry rose superior to all speakers. His close of the harangue was as warm and glowing as the beginning was cold and deficient.

The only man, in my memory, whose powers were perfectly suited to all parts of this celebrated harangue, was William Milward, who, from enjoying a full-toned and harmonious pipe, was frequently tempted to sacrifice sense to sound.

On

† Dr. Arbuthnot.   * Cicero's 2d Philippic.

On particular occasions, and in some parts, he was known to be a judicious and accurate speaker. In Mark Antony he had every thing for him which nature could bestow, person, look, voice; his action and address were easy without art, and his deportment, though not absolutely perfect, was far from ungraceful: he opened the preparatory part of the oration in a low but distinct and audible voice; for nothing can atone for the want of articulation; to be heard is the first lesson the actor should be master of; nor can I applaud the apology of Baron, the French Roscius, who, on his opening Racine's Iphigenia in a whispering tone, when called upon by a spectator to speak louder, replied, *if he did he should not act in character*. Milward, I say, began low, and, by gradual progress, rose to such a height, as not only to inflame the populace on the stage, but to touch the audience with a kind of enthusiastic rapture; when he uttered the following lines:

>————But were I Brutus,
>And Brutus Antony, there were an Antony
>Would ruffle up your spirits, and put a tongue
>In every wound of Cæsar, that should move
>The stones of Rome to rise and mutiny.

It is scarcely to be conceived with what acclamations of applause this was accompanied.

Act IV. Scene III.

Brutus and Cassius.

BRUTUS.

Did not great Julius bleed for justice sake?
What *villain* touch'd his body, that did stab,
And not for justice?

By the word *villain*, a reader, not upon his guard, might be induced to suppose that Brutus termed himself and the rest of the conspirators a band of assassins; but his meaning is, that the lowest in rank amongst them all was actuated, in the killing of Cæsar, with motives of humanity and justice, in ridding the world of a plunderer and a robber.

CASSIUS.

Brutus, *bay* not me.

The old editions read *baite*, but *bay* has a peculiar and adapted sense here; *do not bark and snap at me, like a dog, with your biting language.* Baying is likewise a term applied to a deer, who, when hard run, turns upon the hounds.

IDEM.

———Abler than yourself.
To make conditions.

Dr. Johnson supposes this boast of Cassius to be from a superior knowledge to confer offices at his disposal.

If this refers to Lucius Pella, it will not hold; for he was an officer of Brutus, according to Shakspeare's original, Plutarch; but I think the
author

author meant something more than this, which is but a mean accomplishment for one who stiles himself a better soldier than his brother officer; I imagine it refers to the whole art military, whose various operations he presumes to understand much better than Brutus.

CASSIUS.

———————What, durst not tempt him?

BRUTUS.

For your life, you durst not.

In this last line of Brutus, the actors, from time immemorial, have made a small alteration, which I suppose they imagined would convey the sentiment with stronger emphasis, and make a deeper impression on their auditors. Brutus said, instead of

For your *life*, you durst not,
No, for your *soul*, you durst not.

It must not be forgotten that both their tempers are wrought up to the highest pitch; Cassius to extreme anger and rage, and Brutus to a very warm, though assumedly calm, resolution; their swords are half drawn, and their hilts should meet and repel each other. Quin spoke, *No, for your soul*, &c. with a look of anger approaching to rage. Booth, on the contrary, looking stedfastly at Cassius pronounced the words with firmness indeed, but not raised much above a whisper, which had much greater weight with the spectators, and produced a stronger effect, than the loudness of Quin.

CASSIUS.

———Within, a heart,
Dearer than Plutus' mine, richer than gold;
If that thou *be'ſt a Roman*, take it forth.

If thou art a Roman of the old ſtamp, reſembling Lucius Junius Brutus, thy great anceſtor, rigidly virtuous and inflexibly ſevere, ſuch an one as never knew what it was to pardon the leaſt deviation from right, here is my breaſt, take out my heart. This ſeems to be the meaning of Caſſius's warm and paſſionate offer.

BRUTUS.

When I ſpoke this I was ill-temper'd too.

Here we diſcover the real cauſe of Brutus's ſeverity to his friend: his own diſtreſs of mind and ruffled temper produced the pointed and animated declamation againſt the mercenary behaviour of Caſſius. This is generally the caſe; when friends fall out, the cauſe for quarrel is often juſt, but the immediate incentive to anger often proceeds from ſomething that is remote from it. The mind of Brutus was diſturbed by private calamity, he had juſt received letters acquainting him with the death of his beloved Portia. Caſſius came in his way, and, by provoking a quarrel, brought on himſelf an acrimonious though juſt reprehenſion of his corrupt and venal conduct. Caſſius juſtly merited all the reproaches of his friend; in his government of Syria he was infamouſly rapacious and oppreſſive.

IDEM.

No man bears ſorrow better.——Portia is dead!

Quin's look and tone of voice, in uttering *Portia is dead!* were extremely affecting: his
expreſſive

expressive pause before he spoke fixed the audience in deep attention.

This scene between Brutus and Cassius was the admiration of the age in which the author lived, and has maintained its important character to this hour. But, such was the delicacy of a Frenchman, abbé le Blanc, who resided a few years in this country, and wrote some letters on our customs and manners, that, in his account of Shakspeare's Julius Cæsar, he acquaints his friend that the two great Roman generals upbraided each other in the language of porters; Garrick assured me that when he was in France he refused an invitation to meet this author, on account of his profanation of Shakspeare.

I will not pretend to say that the quarrel between Amintor and Melantius, in the Maid's Tragedy, is an imitation of Shakspeare; the time when that play was first acted is unknown, the merit of that composition is great, the passions are worked up from such incidents as arise from the plot and the situation of the characters; it is impossible to read it without being strongly affected; but, however meritorious it may be, it does not rise to the supreme excellency of the scene between the *half-sworded Romans*.

In Dryden's Troilus and Cressida, the two brothers, Hector and Troilus, quarrel with great vehemence; the occasion is interesting. Love and honour never appeared to more advantage than in this animated scene; the passions have their full vent, and the close is pleasingly affecting. Dryden has the entire merit of it, there being no hint of it in the original. But, when we have said the best we can of it, still art predominates over nature.

I am

I am still more pleased with the same author's interview between Mark Antony and Ventidius, where the honest hardy veteran strives to rouse his emperor and friend from his indolence and dispondence, and awaken him to a sense of honour. The combat between conscious shame and acknowledgment of error is nobly fought, nor do I think any thing in all Dryden's plays so truly dramatic as this. Had such a masterly scene, instead of being placed in the first, been reserved to the fourth or fifth act, All for Love would have challenged immortality; but, not being supported by any thing equal in the succeeding parts of the play, it is now generally neglected.

But Dryden valued himself more highly on the reconciliation-scene between Dorax and Sebastian in the play of that name; and I believe that the tragedy was written for the sake of the sentiments introduced in it. But the upbraidings of Dorax to his royal master are coarse, indecent, and brutal. Who can be interested greatly for a man who turns a rebel to his prince and an apostate to his faith, because a rival courtier is preferred to him? Many elevated thoughts with some warm conflicts of passion, we must allow, the scene does not want. But there is in it too much swell of diction, and too great parade and pomp of action; nature is stifled by art, and art too discernible.

The only scene which in my opinion can be compared with that of Shakspeare's Brutus and Cassius, for natural dialogue and truth of passion, is that admirable one between Agamemnon and Menelaus in the Iphigenia in Aulis, of Euripides. The story is well known. The Grecian fleet is detained at Aulis by contrary winds: Calchas
declares

declares Diana will not grant a fair wind unless the general's daughter is sacrificed to her. Agamemnon sends for Iphigenia, under the pretence of matching her to Achilles; but afterwards, in the distraction of paternal feelings, he dispatches a trusty messenger to forbid her coming. Menelaus meets the servant and forces the letter from him. He upbraids his brother in the sharpest terms for his duplicity; the quarrel proceeds to extremity; when, on a sudden, a messenger enters, and acquaints Agamemnon that Clytemnestra and Iphigenia are just arrived. The distress of the father rouses all the affection of Menelaus, who, after silently contemplating the sufferings of his unhappy brother, approaches him with unspeakable tenderness, and begs his hand.

Αδελφε, δος μοι δεξιας της σης διγειν.

The last act of Julius Cæsar has nothing either in action or sentiment that is very remarkable. Mark Antony's character of Brutus has been often quoted and much celebrated.

> This was the noblest Roman of them all:
> All the conspirators, save only he,
> Did that they did in envy of great Cæsar;
> He only, in a general good to all, made one of them:
> His life was gentle, and the elements
> So mix'd in him, that nature might stand up
> And say to all the world, " this was a man". *

Brutus was extremely unfit to be a ring-leader in a conspiracy; his amiable and gentle spirit could not encounter the rough and thorny business

---

* It must be confessed that Brutus, after the battle of Pharsalia, too hastily forsook the cause he had espoused: he not only made his peace immediately with Cæsar; but, by his advice, the conqueror determined to follow Pompey into Ægypt.

ness necessary to bring about a revolution in the state. The times he lived in were too degenerate and corrupt for so mild a reformer. His great ancestor, Lucius Junius Brutus, could not have effected, in the days of Cæsar, what his hardy virtue and persevering spirit so nobly accomplished in an age undebauched by luxury.

Julius Cæsar, though now laid aside and almost forgotten, was long the favourite of an English audience; though the subject did not invite Shakspeare to ascend *the brightest heaven of his invention*, though it afforded no place for magical inchantment, nor any strong and powerful exhibition of the tumultuous or softer passions of the heart, yet the poet has kept faithfully to the object he had in view. Roman manners and characters are represented with great energy and gravity of sentiment, with superior grace and dignity of action. The hot and selfish Cassius is finely contrasted with the philosophic and generous Brutus. The art of Mark Antony is skilfully unfolded; his oration over the dead body of Cæsar is such a masterpiece of eloquence as is not to be matched in any play antient or modern.

For a more complete view of the merits of this tragedy, I must refer my reader to the judicious remarks of the accomplished Mrs. Montague, in her excellent Essay on the Genius and Writings of Shakspeare.

King

King Lear.

CHAP. XXXI.

Tragedy of Lear *supposed not to be originally much admired.—Fewer editions of it than many of Shakspeare's other plays.—Leonard Diggs.—Downs— Lear not often acted in its pristine state.—Tate's vanity.—Mr. Colman's Lear.—Tate's scenes of Edgar and Cordelia.—Addison's and Richardson's judgment of Lear's catastrophe—Dr. Johnson.— Count Ugolino.—Sir Joshua Reynolds.—Garrick. —Lear's fool.—Woodward.—*Passage *explained.. —Scene judiciously restored by Mr. Colman.—The bastard.—Savage. — His Poem. — Mr. Steevens, Dr. Warburton, and Vanini.—*Unstate myself *explained.—*Old fools are babes, &c. *discussed. Character of the gentleman-usher.—*Lear *not a favourite of the audience in former times.—Booth. Wilks, Mrs. Booth, and Boheme. — Macklin's opinion of Boheme's* Lear.—*His person, voice, and manner.—Print to Mariamne.—Mrs. Seymour.— Quin's Lear.—Booth in uttering Lear's curse inferior to Garrick.—Powell's Lear.—Meaning of some passages.—*Sop of moon shine.—Barbermonger.—Enormous state, &c.—*The superior worth of Kent's character.—Winstone.—Bransby. —Sparks.—Mr. Horne Tooke.—Clarke.—Edgar's disguise.—Tricks of old impostors —Garrick's happy restoration of a passage.—*Tenderhefted *explained.—Worthless pensioners.*

NOT-

NOTWITHSTANDING the tragedy of King Lear is universally esteemed to be one of Shakspeare's noblest productions, I cannot help suspecting that it was not held in equal regard, or at least not so much followed, when first brought on the stage, as many other of our author's pieces which are not superior to it in merit. Mr. Steevens speaks only of two editions of Lear in quarto, prior to the editions of our author's works in folio, 1623. Many of his less perfect efforts were given to the public five or six times before the publication of the folio. None of his contemporaries, who have come down to us have mentioned this masterpiece of plot, passion, and moral. If any traces of that kind could have been found, the accurate Mr. Malone would have inserted them in his new-raised monument to the memory of Shakspeare, the large supplement to his works. Leonard Diggs, in a rapturous vision, prophesied eternity to our author in the following lines prefixed to the *edition of Hemmings and Condell:*

——————This book,
When Brass and marble fade, shall make thee look
Fresh to all ages, when posterity
Shall lothe what's new, think all is prodigy
That is not Shakspeare's.——

And, in another copy of verses, prefixed to his poems, in which the same author has pointed out six or seven of his principal characters, he has taken no notice of Lear: however, as he has likewise omitted others of great importance, I shall not insist upon an argument so very uncertain. Downs, in his Roscius

cius Anglicanus, will enable me to go farther, and upon safer ground. He tells us that, about the year 1663, King Lear was acted, at the Duke's Theatre, *as Shakspeare wrote it.* The principal character was doubtless represented by Betterton, he being at the head of the company. But Downs is silent as to the effect produced by this play; though he enlarges somewhat upon the Othello of Hart, and more upon the Hamlet and Henry VIII. of Betterton. The success of Macbeth is also particularized by this stage-historian. It should seem then that even the action of a Betterton could not support a play, with a catastrophe so shocking and terrible to human nature.

That Lear in its pristine state was not often represented, soon after the restoration, we may then reasonably infer from Downs: and, till Tate produced his alteration of this play, it had to all appearance been laid aside and neglected as unprofitable to the players. Tate himself seems to have been a stranger to its merit till he had examined it, and found a new-discovered treasure of jewels unstrung and unpolished, as he ostentatiously informs us. Though the man is to be laughed at for his vanity, in pretending to mend Shakspeare, and, especially for claiming the play as his own, which he does in the title to one of his pieces; yet, it must be confessed, that weak as he is, he has rescued the play from that oblivion to which the actors had consigned it.

Mr. Colman has within these few years printed an altered Lear of his own, with many judicious restorations from the original copy. I heartily wish he had not taken such a dislike to

the

the passion of Edgar for Cordelia; he would have rescued that love-plan, which I think a good one, from meaner hands, and given a new lustre to the play. Even Mr. Colman was, after mature deliberation, obliged to make Lear end happily. The lovers of Cordelia in the old play do not surely make a more respectable figure than Edgar; Burgundy is just shewn to be despised. The King of France too had sojourned long in the court of Lear, and, though he displays a generous concern for Cordelia's unfortunate situation, he seems to have made no previous declaration of his passion to her, the lady likewise manifests no other regard for him than giving her hand and complying with her destiny. The passion of Edgar and Cordelia is happily imagined; it strongly connects the main plot of the play, and renders it more interesting to the spectators; without this, and the consequent happy catastrophe, the alteration of Lear would have been of little worth; besides, after those turbulent scenes of resentment, violence, disobedience, ingratitude, and rage, between Lear and his two eldest daughters, with the king's consequent agony and distraction, the unexpected interview of Cordelia and Edgar in act III. gives a pause of relief to the harrassed and distressed minds of the audience. It is a gleam of sunshine and a promise of fair weather in the midst of storm and tempest. I have seen this play represented twenty or thirty times, yet I can truly affirm that the spectators always dismissed the two lovers with the most rapturous applause. Besides, it should be observed, that, without such an intervention as this, the action of the play would fall too heavily upon Lear, who stands in need of all the relief which the

conduct

conduct of the fable can afford him. As a writer of plays, a scholar, and critic, I will not compare Mr. Garrick to Mr. Colman; as a man experienced in the conduct of a theatre, and one who well understood what would best please the taste of an audience, I must suppose him equal if not superior to all competition. He long considered the advantages and disadvantages which might flow from the exclusion or the retaining the scenes of Tate in question; and, after well-weighed reflection, he thought proper to preserve the greatest part of them.

The judgment of Addison, who has flatly given his opinion against Tate's alteration of the catastrophe, is not to be implicitly relied on. In an essay or two in the Spectator, concerning dramatic writing and poetical justice, this excellent author has taken the melancholy side of the question, and is in my opinion too great an advocate for the poisoned bowl and the bloody dagger.

The pathetic Richardson, in his Clarissa, has embraced Addison's opinion, relative to the catastrophe of Lear. I shall beg leave to oppose to these writers the judgment of one, whose superiority in critical knowledge is universally allowed: Dr. Johnson observes, that a play, in which the wicked prosper and the virtuous miscarry, may doubtless be good, because it is a just representation of the common events of human life; but since, says this writer, all reasonable beings naturally love justice, I cannot easily be persuaded, that the observation of justice makes a play worse, or that, if other excellences are equal, the audience will not always rise better pleased from the final triumph of persecuted virtue. He proceeds to say that, in the present case, the public has decided; Cordelia, from the time of Tate, has always

ways retired with victory and felicity. He farther says, that, many years ago, he was so shocked by Cordelia's death, that he knows not whether he ever endured to read again the last scenes of the play till he undertook to revise them as an editor. *Johnson and Steevens's Shakspeare,* vol. IX. p. 566. *last edition.*

If these scenes are really so afflicting to a mind of sensibility in the closet, what would they produce in action? What exquisite grief and unutterable horror would such a painter as Garrick, in the last scene of the play, have raised in the breast of a spectator? Who can endure to look for any considerable time at the agonizing woe in the countenance of Count Ugolino, drawn by the inimitable pencil of Reynolds? But were you to produce that subject on the stage, in action, none but a heart of marble could sustain it. The catastrophes of Shakspeare and Tate are strongly marked in the following lines, spoken by Edgar to Albany, in the last act of the play:

> This would have seem'd a period
> To such as love not sorrow.

That is, *such as do not love to feed upon melancholy.*

> —— But another,
> To amplify too much, would make much more,
> And top extremity.

For *such people the cup of bitterness must overflow to please them.*

The cruel never shed tears, it is true, but to be continually weeping is more than humanity can bear. The slaughter of characters in the last act of the old Lear too much resembles the conclusion of Tom Thumb; for no man of any consequence is left alive except Albany and Edgar.

It was once in contemplation with Mr. Garrick to restore the part of the fool, which he designed for Woodward, who promised to be very chaste in his colouring, and not to counteract the agonies of Lear: but the manager would not hazard so bold an attempt; he feared, with Mr. Colman, that the feelings of Lear would derive no advantage from the buffooneries of the parti-coloured jester.*

FRANCE.

————Sure her offence
Must be of such unnatural degree
That monsters it; or your fore-vouch'd affection
Fall into taint.

The King of France does by no means charge Lear with vouching affection for Cordelia, which he did not feel, as Dr. Johnson seems to interpret the passage: his meaning is, that either she, who was so lately your darling and your dearest child, must have committed some enormous offence, or you must be censured for placing your affections upon one who did not possess those qualities which your fondness has attributed to her.

After the King has returned with Burgundy and France, and a short conversation between Cordelia and her two elder sisters has taken place, Shakspeare

* In all probability, Nokes, *whose face was a comedy*, acted the Fool with Betterton's Lear: if so, we may guess the consequence.

Shakſpeare thought proper to prepare the audience for the outrageous acts of diſobedience and cruelty, committed by Goneril and Regan againſt their father, in a ſhort ſcene, wherein the tempers of the two ladies are unfolded, and their intention to be conjunct in the treatment of their father declared; this neceſſary dialogue Mr. Colman has judiciouſly preſerved, but it eſcaped the diligence of Mr. Garrick.

Scene II. Edmund's ſoliloquy.

EDMUND.

Thou, Nature, art my goddeſs!
———Why *baſtard?* wherefore *baſe?*
Who, in the luſty ſtealth of nature, take
More compoſition and fierce quality
Than doth within a dull, ſtale, tir'd, bed
Go to the creating of a whole tribe of fops,
Got 'tween aſleep and wake!

Some of the warmeſt and moſt poetical lines, in Savage's poem of the Baſtard, are little more than a paraphraſe of Edmund's ſoliloquy.

Bleſt be the baſtard's birth, through won'drous ways
He ſhines excentric like the comet's blaze;
No ſickly fruit of faint compliance he,
He's ſtamp'd in nature's mint with extacy;
He lives to build, not boaſt, a generous race,
No tenth tranſmitter of a fooliſh face,
He kindling from within requires no flame,
He glories in a baſtard's glowing name.

In the Revenger's Tragedy, first printed in 1607, Spurio, the Bastard, says,

———Adultery is my nature;
Faith, if the truth were known, I was begot
After some gluttonous dinner, some stirring dish
Was my first father, when deep healths went round,
And ladies cheeks were painted red with wine,
Their tongues, as short and nimble as their heels,
Uttering words sweet and thick. *

Mr. Steevens justly refutes Dr. Warburton's opinion of Shakspeare's intending to make Edmund a confirmed atheist. The strange wish of Vanini, that he had been born a bastard, which the doctor has quoted in his notes on Edmund's speech of bastardy, and contains something very like Shakspeare, is brought to prove the divinity of our poet's genius, which foretold (as it were) what such an atheist as Vanini would say. With submission, this is all gratis dictum. The reader of this soliloquy may easily perceive that Edmund sufficiently feels the disgrace of illegitimacy, but that he is willing to make the best of it, and affects to embrace that with a hearty good-will, which he would fain, if in his power, throw aside; and this is human nature: how many affect to be fond of, or laugh at, a blemish of birth, or an accident of time, which they cannot avoid? Shakspeare makes Richard the Third talk with unconcern of his crooked back and bandy legs, and take pleasure in *descanting on his own deformity.*

GLOSTER.

* Vide Mr. Reed's accurate edition of Dodsley's old plays, vol. IV.

GLOSTER.

I would unstate myself to be in a due resolution.

I cannot be convinced that any of the commentators have given a proper solution of the word *unstate*.

The Earl, between his regard for a son whom he tenderly loves, and the evidence produced by Edmund of his disobedience and undutiful behaviour, is in a state of perplexity and the most doubtful anxiety. Therefore he intreats Edmund to make use of all his art and contrivance to discover the real disposition of Edgar. To obtain the knowledge of this truth he makes use of an expression which is of the same import with one often used upon similar, or indeed slighter, occasions. " To know the truth of this or that mat-
" ter, I would give all I am worth in the world;
" for then I shall know what to do." And this is, I think, the true meaning of *unstate myself to be in a due resolution*.

Scene III.

GONERIL.

―――Now, by my life,
Old fools are babes again, and must be us'd
With checks, as flatteries, when they are seen, abus'd.

Two notes of some length are employed upon this passage by Dr. Warburton and Dr. Johnson, neither of which is satisfactory: the last commentator indeed seems to imagine that the author did not think these lines worth his correcting, and for that reason threw them away: but, this is getting rid of a difficulty at the expence of the poet.

poet. I think the following explanation will get something like sense out of these obscure lines:

Old people, says Goneril, when turned to dotage, must be managed with the same controul, and checked in the same manner we do gross flatterers, who overshoot the mark. The first are peevish and troublesome from decay of their faculties, and the others are offensive from their want of discretion.

Act I. Scene IV.

Enter Steward, or Oswald.

The Steward is a necessary implement employed by the poet to carry on the plot: I have seen it acted by several eminent players, Yates, Shuter, King, Dodd, &c. but the character is so distasteful, and by the comedians falsely supposed to be unimportant, that all of them, of any note, no sooner get into the part but they grow tired and withdraw from it. He generally enters the stage in a careless disengaged manner, humming a tune, as if on purpose to give umbrage to the King by his neglect of him. Vernon was impudently negligent and characteristically provoking in Oswald; however he grew too great for the part; and it is now acted by an inferior player.

STEWARD.

I'll not be struck, my lord!

KENT.

Nor tript neither, you *base foot-ball player*.

By

By this low term of *base foot-ball player* Kent means, that *he resembles a fellow who, in endeavouring to kick the bladder or ball, misses his aim and tumbles down.*

GONERIL.

———Put it on
By your allowance.

Encourage it by your authority.

IDEM.

———More like a tavern, or a brothel,
Than a grac'd palace.

More resembling a house of disorderly entertainment than the residence of a prince, where all things should be managed with order, grace, and decorum.

LEAR.

Hear, nature, dear goddess, hear a father!

Much has been said by Downs, by the Tatler, by Cibber, and others, of Betterton's uncommon powers of action and utterance in several of Shakspeare's principal parts, particularly Hamlet, Macbeth, Othello, and Brutus, but no writer has taken notice of his exhibition of Lear; a part of equal consequence, and requiring as perfect skill in the player as any of them. I am almost tempted to believe that this tragedy, notwithstanding that Tate's alterations were approved, was not in such an equal degree of favour, with the public, as Hamlet, Othello, and many other of our poet's dramas. The Spectators, when they were first published, contained

I 4 theatrical

theatrical advertisements, but no Lear is, I believe, to be found amongst them; had it been a favourite tragedy, Wilks, after the death of Betterton, would, in all probability, have seized Lear for his friend John Mills; and this would have served the double purpose of elevating his favourite and of depressing Booth, whose pretensions to the character were more just. It is in vain, therefore, to talk of Betterton's Lear, for we know nothing of it. After Booth became Wilks's brother-manager, he could then talk to him as an equal, and claim such parts as were due to his merit: and, some time after he had acquired a share in the patent, he undertook the representation of Lear, and was much admired in it. His Cordelia was Mrs. Booth; she was well suited, by the agreeableness of her person, her voice, and manner of speaking, to several of the soft and gentler females, such as Ophelia in Hamlet, and Selima in Tamerlane: however, I think she was rather a cold actress in tragedy; in comedy she displayed a pleasing vivacity and elegant deportment, that charmed the public long; in the Harriet of Etherege's Sir Fopling Flutter she sang some of the London cries very agreeably; but her chief excellence consisted in a graceful manner of dancing. It was said of Booth, who would sometimes act lazily, that Lear was one of those parts which he never slighted. But, however excellent Booth's performance of this character was, he had no mean competitor in a young actor, who, from small beginnings, rose to a very high degree of estimation with the public.

Anthony Boheme was first taken notice of at some booth, either in Bartholomew or Southwark

wark fair, for a manner of speaking and acting superior to his situation. Mr. Rich employed him first at a very low salary, but his great merit soon increased his income. As he was an original actor and not an auricular imitator, his manner of acting Lear was very different from that of Booth. Mr. Macklin speaks of Boheme's stage-abilities with great approbation. To his Lear he gave a trait, he says, of the antique. In his person he was tall, his features were expressive, with something of the venerable cast, which gave force and authority to the various situations and passions of the character; the tones of his voice very equally powerful and harmonious, and his whole action suited to the age and feelings of Lear. I never saw a portrait of this very valuable comedian. But there is an engraving to the second edition of Mariamne, by Vertue, from a drawing of his own, which exhibited some of the principal characters in that tragedy, and not unlike the actors who represented them, particularly Herod and Mariamne by Boheme and Mrs. Seymour. The figure and countenance of Boheme appears majestic and expressive. Quin, who had acted Gloster in the same play many years with great approbation of the public, was after the death of Boheme, persuaded to try his abilities in Lear. No less than twenty-two rehearsals were demanded by him; but he, being at that time young and dissipated, attended only two of them. He fell infinitely short of his predecessor in almost every scene of Lear. Quin felt neither the tender nor the violent emotions of the soul, and therefore should not have hazarded his reputation in a part for which nature unfitted him. However, as he was a man of undeniable merit

merit and an excellent speaker, he did not so entirely offend as to throw himself out of public favour. Booth, who was an actor of genius, and though a professed admirer of Betterton almost to idolatry, had too much judgment to copy or servilely imitate his action. He has been known to read a scene in a part, acted by Betterton, in that great actor's manner, to the admiration of his hearers; but, when asked why he would not so represent a character throughout, his constant answer was, that it was too much for him. He stole what he could from his great exemplar, and fitted it to his own powers and manner, just as that agreeable actor, William Powell, did by Garrick. In uttering the imprecation on Goneril, Booth was more rapid than Garrick, his fire was ardent and his feelings were remarkably energetic, but they were not attended with those strugglings of parental affection, and those powerful emotions of conflicting passions, so visible in every look, action, and attitude, of our great Roscius. I have heard certain critics complain, that, in pronouncing this denunciation, Garrick was too deliberate, and not so quick in the emission of his words as he ought to have been; that he did not yield to that impetuosity which his particular situation required. But we should reflect, that Lear is not agitated by one passion only, that he is not moved by rage, by grief, and indignation, singly, but by a tumultuous combination of them all together, where all claim to be heard at once, and where one naturally interrupts the progress of the other. Besides, the lines are so full of rich and distinct matter, that few men can roll them off with any degree of swiftness.

Shakspeare,

Shakspeare, we should consider, too, wrote them for the mouth of one who was to assume the action of an old man of fourscore, for a father as well as a monarch, in whom the most bitter execrations are accompanied with extreme anguish, with deep sighs, and involuntary tears. Garrick rendered the curse so terribly affecting to the audience, that, during his utterance of it, they seemed to shrink from it as from a blast of lightning. His preparation for it was extremely affecting; his throwing away his crutch, kneeling on one knee, clasping his hands together, and lifting his eyes towards heaven, presented a picture worthy the pencil of a Raphael.

In Barry's personating Lear, his figure was dignified and venerable: his manner of speaking this celebrated imprecation was impressive; but his voice wanted that power and flexibility which varied passion requires. His pauses and broken interruptions of speech, of which he was extremely enamoured, sometimes to a degree of impropriety, were at times too inartificially repeated; nor did he give that terror to the whole which the great poet intended should predominate.

Powell's King Lear ought not to be forgotten, it was a fair promise of something great in future. He had about him the blossoms of an excellent actor; many scenes of the choleric king were well adapted to his fine conceptions of the passions, and especially those of the softer kind. Had he lived till now we should not have regretted quite so much the loss of our great tragic actors, Garrick and Barry.

Dr.

Dr. Franklin thinks nothing can exceed the bitterness of OEdipus's execration of his two sons, except perhaps the curse of Lear on his daughter: from the following extract the reader may perhaps determine.

OEDIPUS.

―――Meantime, thou worst,
Thou most abandoned of the sons of men,
Be gone away, and with thee bear this curse
Which here I do pronounce: To Argus ne'er
May'ft thou return! never may Thebes be thine!
Soon may'ft thou perish by a brother's hand!
Slaying the flayer! may dark Erebus
Receive them both! And now on you I call,
Ye goddeffes rever'd! and thou, O Mars!
Thou, who haft rais'd the bitter strife between
My impious sons, bear witness to my words!

Franklin's translation of Sophocles's
OEdipus Coloneus.

In Lear's curse there are two or three passages on which I shall offer something.

LEAR.

Create her *child of spleen!*

That is, *malicious* and *disobedient*.

IDEM.

―――That it may live
And prove a thwart disnatured torment to her!

Something like this is to be found in the execration pronounced on sacrilegious persons amongst the Greeks.

IDEM.

IDEM.

The *untented* woundings of a father's curse
Pierce every sense about thee!

The incurable execrations of a parent. The curses of parents amongst the ancients were greatly dreaded, for they were supposed to be always fulfilled.

Act II.

EDMUND.

In cunning I must draw my sword upon you.

I must seem to be your enemy, though I am not, lest my father should suspect me to be in confederacy with you.

Scene VI.

REGAN.

Threading dark night.

This is a metaphor plainly borrowed from the threading of a needle. Our business, says Regan, is of such importance, that it obliges us to travel by night, though it be as difficult to keep the right road in darkness as it is to hit the eye of a needle without a steady hand and a proper thread. This I think is our author's meaning.

Kent and Oswald.

This incident of a quarrel between the two messengers from Lear and Goneril is admirably contrived to advance the business or plot of the play, it con-

contributes to open the character of Regan more at large, and of Cornwall, who was hitherto unknown: it also prepares the reader for the grand scene of terror which concludes act II.

KENT.

I'll make a sop of the moonshine of you.

This was in all probability, in Shakspeare's days, a proverbial expression. A mouthful of moonshine was first introduced, I believe, into conversation, by a member of the Irish Parliament, soon after the revolution: this signifies *a bite at a shadow:* by the other, Kent means, that, *by the help of the moon, he will dispatch him as quickly as he would eat a morsel of bread.*

IDEM.

You *neat* slave!

Mr. Steevens has interpreted the word *neat* very justly by *finical,* which is a certain impertinence in dress and behaviour.

Neatness itself impertinent in him.   POPE.

This is farther explained above by glass-gazing, and this too will help us to the meaning, if I mistake not, of barber-monger, a fellow, whose hair is powdered and curled most exactly; what the French term *bien poudré.* So Mark Antony, when most completely prepared by dress to meet Cleopatra, is said by Ænobarbus to be *barber'd all o'er.*

IDEM.

IDEM.

Thou whoreson zed, thou unnecessary letter.

Unnecessary because compounded of two other letters, *S, D.* Grammarians tell us the Doric Zeta is composed of these two letters.

IDEM.

Spare my grey beard, you *wag-tail*.

This word is of the same signification, I believe, as *bob-tail*, which is a cant term for an eunuch or any impotent person. Shakspeare makes this Oswald an abstract of all vices of the worst kind, and perhaps he might mean the same thing as Juvenal does by the word *ceventem*.

———Ego te *ceventem*, Sexte, verebor?

Juvenal Sat. II.

REGAN.

These kind of knaves I know, which in their plainness
Harbour more craft and more corrupter ends
Than twenty silly ducking observants
Who stretch their duties nicely.

The fellow who affects the character of a plain downright man, who calls himself John Blunt, is more to be guarded against than the supple flatterer, who watches your looks to shew his ready obedience to your commands, and stretches his duty to a ridiculous excess to gain some reward for his pains.

Regan admits that both characters are worthless, but the latter, she says, is far less dangerous than the former.

KENT.

KENT.

―――― None of these rogues and cowards,
But Ajax is their sport.

The brave plain honest man is the butt of the most despicable wretches.

IDEM.

―――― Nothing almost sees miracles.
But misery.――――

That is, misfortune is industrious, and is ever on the watch, and discovers that, to which busy prosperity cannot attend.

KENT [READING A LETTER.]

―――― And shall find time,
From this *enormous state*—seeking to give
Remedies.――――

Kent, upon looking on the letter from Cordelia, says that she has been informed of his course. Cordelia could have possibly learned no more, than that the generous Kent had disguised himself to serve at all hazards his injured master, together with the insolent behaviour of Goneril to her father. Regan had not as yet seen Lear; consequently her conduct could not be arraigned by the name of *enormous rule*, as Mr. Steevens imagines; nor could Cordelia know what passed in this last scene. Dr. Johnson has rightly interpreted the word *enormous* by *something unwonted and out of rule*. Cordelia plainly intimates, that as soon as she could disburthen herself from that weight of pomp and ceremony which attended her new dignity of queen of France, she would

would immediately endeavour to correct those evils which the ungrateful and wicked conduct of Goneril had brought upon her father.

It is the peculiar privilege of Shakspeare to draw characters of the most singular form, and such as, though acknowledged to come from nature's mint, had never entered into the mind of any other writer, antient or modern. This man combined, in his imagination, all the possibilities of human action with all the varieties of situation and passion. It is in this wonderful creative faculty that he excels all dramatic writers. He alone seems to have discerned how far the exercise of the noblest qualities of the mind could and ought to proceed. The generosity of Kent is not to be matched in any other drama, antient or modern. The man who has the courage, in the face of a court, to reprove his prince for an act of folly, violence, and injustice, after being condemned by him to perpetual banishment for his honest freedom, apprehensive lest some ill consequences should attend his master's rash conduct, assumes a mean disguise with no other view than to serve him in his utmost need, to wait upon him as his menial servant, and to do him all servile offices his necessities should require. No man will think so meanly of human nature as not to acknowledge that virtue so disinterested is the growth of humanity. None but a Shakspeare ever conceived so noble an example of persisting goodness and generous fidelity.

The name of the comedian who originally represented Kent is as much unknown as that of any other early performer in the tragedy. Winstone, a man of rather large bulk, harsh features, and

and a rough loud voice, who, about thirty years since, acted Kent when Garrick was the Lear, had a good deal of that manly boldness which is one striking trait of the part, more especially when he first puts on the disguise; but he could not equally assume the generous feelings of the sympathizing friend, who suffered more in his mind than did his unhappy and distressed old master. Bransby, his successor, more happily expressed that affectionate humanity which is the brightest part of Kent's character. Bransby was spirited without being boisterous, and blunt without vulgarity. Luke Sparks had likewise considerable merit in this part. Luke, though no scholar, was a man of strong intelligence, and knew how to take possession of a character, but he sometimes gave too much hardness to his manner, his colouring was coarse, though his outline was generally exact. I am pleased to find that no actor has copied the particular step of Sparks, which he too often enlarged into a strut. Sparks acquired a competent fortune, though, I believe, not entirely from acting. He retired from the stage about twenty years since, and lived at Brentford. He died about sixteen years ago; and, with his almost dying breath, begged that the funeral service might be pronounced over him by Mr. Horne, now Mr. Horne-Tooke. Mr. Clarke is at present a very respectable representer of Kent's honest fervour and generous fidelity.

Scene

KING LEAR.   189

Scene III.

EDGAR, [SOLUS.]

——My face I will begrime with filth.

It was the custom with cheating beggars formerly, and, I believe, is not yet out of practice with them, to raise artificial sores on their bodies to move compassion, by burning crow's-foot, spearwort, and salt, together, and, clapping them at once on the face, it fretted the skin; then, with a linen rag, which sticks close, they tear off the skin and strew on a little powder of arsenic which gives it an ugly and ill-favoured look: these sores are, in the canting phrase, called *clegms*.

IDEM.

Strike, in their numb'd and mortify'd bare arms,
Pins, wooden pricks, nails, &c.

Hypocrisy is of all nations and all ages. The practice of the religious cheats, in the East Indies, at this day, is to drive a piece of iron thro' some part of the body, which for some time gives great pain to the sufferer: these rascals on this account are held so sacred that nobody dares offend them.

Scene IV.

LEAR.

Oh! how the mother swells upward to my heart.

So

So in Julius Cæsar, Act IV. Cassius to Brutus.

> Have you not love enough to bear with me,
> When the rash humour, which my mother gave me,
> Makes me forgetful?———

LEAR.

> Do you but mark, how this becomes the house?
> Dear daughter, I confess that I am old;
> Age is unnecessary: on my knees I beg,
> That you'll vouchsafe me raiment, bed, and food.

This presents to the spectator a most striking picture of an unhappy aged parent, who finds himself reduced to the necessity of representing, in his own person, by action, the absurdity, as well as wickedness, of his childrens conduct to him. This was a dramatic situation utterly unknown to Booth, Boheme, and Quin, because this affecting passage was omitted in Tate's alteration of Lear. It was happily restored by Mr. Garrick, who knew its beauty. He threw himself on both knees, with his hands clasped, and, in a supplicating tone, repeated this touching, though ironical, petition.

IDEM.

Thy *tender-hefted* nature.

By *hefted* Mr. Steevens thinks the author means *heaved*; a bosom agitated by tender passions. I suppose the expression was intended to signify *smooth*, or *soft-handled*, consequently put here for *gentleness of disposition*. Heft or *handled*; Teutonicè *haft*; Belgicè *heft*. *Minshew's Dictionary*.

IDEM.

I D E M.

  Her eyes are fierce, but thine
Do comfort, and not burn.

 Maſſinger, who admired and imitated our author, had this paſſage in his eye in his Baſhful Lover.

  ————Let your beams,
Warm and comfort, not conſume, me.

I D E M.

  ————If your ſweet ſway
Allow obedience.————

 To Mr. Steevens's various quotations, in ſupport of the old reading *allow,* in oppoſition to Dr. Warburton's *hallow,* let us add the deciſive authority of Shakſpeare himſelf, in his Timon of Athens, Act V. where the ſenator tells Alcibaides, that he ſhall be

  Allow'd with abſolute power.

 That is, *Inveſted with ſupreme authority.*

L E A R.

  ————And, 'ſquire-like, penſion beg,
To keep baſe life on foot.————

 To beſtow a penſion on virtue and merit is conferring honour on the donor and receiver, but there ſurely cannot be a meaner character than the man, who, without any ſervice performed to his king and country, maintanis himſelf by a gratuitous income.

IDEM,

IDEM.

——— Touch me with noble anger.

Dr. Warburton is continually making our old bard deeply verſed in antient learning, and particularly in the more abſtruſe parts of mythology. Shakſpeare's meaning in this place is very obvious; let me, ſays Lear, finding himſelf give way to the weakneſs of humanity occaſioned by his daughters unexampled inſolence and cruelty, bear my misfortunes like a king and a man, by requiting diſobedience and ingratitude with wrath, reſentment, and revenge, and not melt into tears, ſighs and womaniſh lamentations.

CHAP.

CHAP. XXXII.

Nuncle.—*Court holy-water.*— *Caitiff.*—*Derived from the Italian.*—*Nero an angler in the infernal regions.*—*Wit borrowed from Lucian.*—*Tom Brown.*—*Deprivation of sight, a Norman punishment.*—*William the Conqueror.*—*Polymnestor and OEdipus.*—*Manner of putting out Gloster's eyes.* —*Gold-beater's skin.*—*Gloster by Quin*—*Berry*— *Davies.*—*Our mean secures us.*—*Lines of Dryden.*—*Slaves heaven's ordinance discussed.*— *Dover cliff.*—I fear your disposition.—*Mistake of Dr. Johnson.*—Better day—*Farther explained.* —*The steward's fidelity.*—*The word* attached. —But to the girdle do the gods inherit.—*Brantome quoted.*—*Edgar generous.*—*Woman's will.*— *The most pathetic of all interviews.*—*Soul in bliss.* — *Purgatory.* — *Greek tragedians.* — *Shakspeare's characters superior to all others.*—*Garrick inimitable.*—*Mrs. Cibber's Cordelia.*—*Mrs. Davies.* — *Burbage and Taylor.* — *Wilks.* — *George Powell.*—*Smith.*—*Ryan.*—*Havard.*—*Reddish. Shakspeare a moralist.*—*Edmund's remorse.*—*Tom Walker.*—*Passages explained.*—*Tate's additional scenes.*—*Garrick's look and action.*—Old Lear shall be a king again.—*Particular respect paid to the tragedy of Lear.*—*Garrick's masterpiece.*— *Three characters.*—*Martyrs to virtue.*—*Story of a young actress.*

FOOL.

FOOL.

O *nuncle*, court holy-water, in a dry house, is better than the rain-water out of door.

*N*UNCLE, or *uncle*, was formerly a provincial term of regard from the lowest of the people to their superiorss and not yet obsolete in some parts of Shropshire, &c. By court holy-water being better than rain-water, the Fool plainly wishes that Lear would return to his daughters; for flattery, he insinuates, is better in a warm house than plain dealing in the midst of a storm.

KENT.

————Man's nature cannot carry
The affliction nor the fear.

It is not in humanity to endure the violence or the affright which attends such a dreadful storm.

LEAR.

Caitiff, shake to pieces.

The commentators derive the word *caitiff* from captive, or the French word *chetiff*. It is perhaps deduced from the Italian word *cativo*, base, wicked, profligate. It is so understood by Berkley in his Ship of Fools:

> That none wise or good will commit this offence;
> For all are *Cayliffes* that are of this lewd sort.

IDEM.

IDEM.

Poor fool and knave, I have one part in my heart
That's sorry yet for thee.

Amidst all his afflictions, Lear recollects that he has brought misfortune and sufferance on those who used to look up to him for protection and kindness. This is one of those happy touches of Shakspeare, where humanity triumphs over selfishness; and, it is to such abundant moral and pathetic applications to our feelings, that he owes a great part of that preference we give him over all other dramatic writers.

Scene VI.

EDGAR.

Fraterreto calls me, and tells me, *Nero* is an angler in the lake of darkness.

This is borrowed from Rabelais; and it is an imitation of him who derived the idea of giving trades to emperors, kings, and other great men, in the infernal regions, fom Lucian. In his Menippus seu Necyomantia, he introduces kings and grandees begging, selling salt-fish, and teaching elements of learning to supply their necessities.

Πολλω δ' αν οιμαι μαλλον εγελας, &c —

" You would have smiled to see some of our kings and satraps turned beggars there, or selling salt-fish for their bread, or teaching school, scoffed at and buffeted like the meanest slaves. I could scarce contain myself when I saw Philip of Macedon there, as they pointed him out to me me in a corner, healing the wounds of old shoes."

Franklin's Lucian, vol. I. 8vo.

This single hint of the great original father of humour has produced innumerable imitations of the smaller wits. Tom Brown is perhaps one of the best as well as most fruitful in this kind of infernal drollery.

GLOSTER.

By the kind gods.

There is no occasion for any ostentation of learning or acuteness here. *Kind* is a general term for good, bounteous, merciful.

CORNWALL.

Upon these eyes of thine I'll set my foot.

In some of the old English plays, written by Marlow, Marston, Ford, and others, we find shocking instances of mutilated limbs, of pulling out eyes, &c. but nothing in all Shakspeare resembling this shocking act of Cornwall. This violence, committed against humanity by the deprivation of sight, was, I think, peculiar to the Normans, and almost unknown to this island till the time of William the Conqueror. Our old historians relate many terrible barbarities committed by this unrelenting and victorious tyrant upon his unhappy English subjects; and, amongst many other species of cruelty, the evulsion of the eyes was not unfrequent. We are told that the purity of the Grecian stage would not permit any transaction of this kind to be brought before the spectators. But the Polymnestor, of Euripides, whose eyes

eyes are put out by Hecuba and her maids, is produced to the audience hideoufly lamenting his misfortune. The blind OEdipus, of Sophocles, in a pathetic addrefs to Creon and the Chorus, recommends his daughters to their care and protection.

No authority, of ancient or later date, will juftify the exhibition of a fpectacle which affrighted nature fhrinks from.——Some very high reward ought to be given to an audience who are obliged to view fo difgufting a fight as a human creature when his eyes are torn from their fockets; voluntarily or involuntarily, it matters not. The cruel and fordid Polymneftor might, indeed, as he deferved, have been punifhed with the lofs of fight, and not have been brought on the ftage afterwards; and difmiffed, like fome of Shakfpeare's characters, when dying, with a prophecy in his mouth. The fpeech of OEdipus, after he has pulled out his eyes, is really affecting, but not of fuch excellence as to recompenfe the fpectators for fo mortifying a fpectacle.

That the tragedy of Lear, as originally written, did not pleafe the audience, when acted, foon after the Reftoration, by Betterton and his company, I have proved, as far as probability will warrant me, by Downs: nor can it be furprizing, that the fpectators fhould be fhocked at fo horrible a fight as one man ftamping upon the eyes of another, and at the fame time encouraged to proceed in his barbarity by one of the fofter fex! After all, Shakfpeare might poffibly contrive not to execute this horrible deed upon the ftage, though it is fo quoted in the book. He was extremely careful of offending the eyes, as well as ears, of the fpectators, by any thing outrageous.

Glofter's

Gloster's losing his eyes is so essential to the plot, that Mr. Colman found it impossible to throw it out. However, at the present, the sufferer is forced into some adjoining room; and the ears of the audience are more hurt by his cries than their eyes can be when he is afterwards led on the stage. The gold-beaters skin, applied to the sockets, as if to staunch the bleeding, abates something perhaps of the hideousness of the spectacle.

I have already said, that Quin was justly celebrated for his performance of Gloster. He was succeeded by Hulet, a man of great merit in the sock and buskin. At Drury-lane, the elder Mills acted Gloster with Booth. Ned Berry, a man of very considerable abilities in a great variety of parts, was Garrick's Gloster for many years.—— His countenance was expressive, his figure large and important, his voice sonorous, and his feelings of passion full and energetic. When sickness deprived the stage of this valuable man, Mr. Garrick called upon the writer of this Miscellany to represent the part of Gloster; the candour of the audience gave him much more encouragement than he expected.

Act IV.

GLOSTER.

————————Full oft 'tis seen
Our *mean* secures us, and our mere defects
Prove our commodities.

Dr. Warburton's *mediocre* and *moderate,* for *mean,* are approved by Mr. Steevens. I should wish to go a little farther than *mediocrity* or *competency.*

tency. Shakſpeare intends, in my opinion, by this term, that ſituation in life which is ſo low as to excite no envy from rivals or fear from ſuperiors. Inſignificancy of character and deficiency in means are often, I believe, according to the mind of Gloſter, real advantages.

If more were neceſſary to eſtabliſh this interpretation of the word *mean,* two lines, attributed to Dryden, in the altered Macbeth, and ſpoken by Macduff when he takes leave of his wife, will, I hope, be deemed not foreign to the purpoſe:

> You to your weakneſs all your ſafety owe,
> As graſs eſcapes the ſcythe by being low.

IDEM.

> Let the ſuperfluous and luſt-dieted man,
> Who *ſlaves heaven's ordinance,* &c.

There cannot, in my opinion, be a happier expreſſion than that of *ſlaving the ordinance of heaven*; though Dr. Warburton would ſubſtitute *brave*; and Dr. Johnſon thinks, *to ſlave an ordinance* may ſignify *to ſlight or ridicule it.* But the contemptuous hypocrite makes the laws of heaven his property; he puts them on for convenience, and throws them aſide for the ſame purpoſe; they are his ſtalking horſe, to reach what he aims at; for this reaſon, they are, with great propriety, termed his *ſlaves,* whom he abuſes at will. Mr. Steevens rightly obſerves, that to *ſlave* an ordinance, is to treat it like a *ſlave,* and make it ſubject to us.

I D E M.

There is a cliff, whose high and bending head
Looks fearfully on the confined deep.

Southern had this passage, probably, in his eye, in the fifth act of Oroonoko:

————Oh! for a whirlwind's wing,
To carry us to yonder cliff, that *frowns*
Upon the flood!

Scene II.

ALBANY, [TO GONERIL.]

I fear your disposition.

When I reflect upon your monstrous ingratitude and cruelty to your indulgent father, I fear lest heaven should dispose of you in such a manner as to make you a terrible example of its vengeance. There cannot be a better commentary, on this text, than the words which fell from one of Cornwall's servants, who had been an eye-witness of Regan's brutal behaviour to Gloster:

—————————If she live long,
And in the end meet the old course of death,
Women will all turn monsters.

MESSENGER.

A servant that he bred, thrill'd with *remorse*—

Remorse, in Shakspeare, generally signifies *pity*, not *compunction*.

GONERIL.

GONERIL.

One way, I like this well.

Dr. Johnson thinks Goneril is pleased that Cornwall is destroyed, who was preparing to make war on her and her husband; but is afraid of losing Edmund to the widow. But, on the contrary, Albany and Cornwall were both united, notwithstanding some small differences, called, by Kent, *snuffs and packings,* between them, against Lear, Cordelia, and their French allies. Goneril's liking might proceed from a suggestion, that it would be no difficult matter to wrest her sister's dominions from her now her husband was removed. If Cornwall died without issue, Goneril was presumptive heiress to Regan.

Scene III.

GENTLEMAN.

―――You have seen
Sunshine and rain at once. Her smiles and tears
Were like a *better day*.

The last editors of Shakspeare have very judiciously abstained from altering an old reading, where sense could be made of it, for a better. Dr. Warburton proposes, instead of *better day,* to substitute *a wetter May,* with much plausibility. Mr. Steevens has well supported the text as it now stands. I beg leave to add, to what that gentleman has advanced, that *the smiles of a better day* is relatively just. For, as days, in the beginning of summer, with a mixture of rain and sunshine, are a pleasing promise of the fruits of the earth to follow; so the tears and smiles of

Cordelia were good omens of her resolution to bring relief and assistance to her father.

Scene V. Regan and Oswald.

Dr. Johnson wonders that Shakspeare should represent the Steward, who is a mere agent of baseness, capable of fidelity. When a man is amply rewarded, for his iniquitous compliances with the commands of his superiors, it is but natural to imagine he will be true to his employers, especially as he will have reason to dread the punishment which would be inflicted for his disobedience. That such a wretch should be anxious, when dying, for the delivery of that letter which he would not suffer to be unsealed, is not very surprising; it was only the consequence of his pursuing the track of his accustomed practice.

EDGAR.

———— ——How fearful
And dizzy 'tis to cast one's eyes so low! &c.

This is a view of Dover-cliff, taken by a man, who assumes affright, which he feels not, in order to raise it in another. In those, who view it now, it does not raise any extraordinary terror; for, in all probability, the altitude is something diminished since the days of Shakspeare. The ascent to it is easy, and the prospect from it nothing alarming.

IDEM.

Ten masts *at each* make not the altitude.

Mr. Pope altered *at each*, to *attach'd*; and Dr. Johnson thinks it may stand, if the word was known

known in our author's time.——Minshew, who published his Dictionary of nine languages in 1617, a year after Shakspeare's death, explains the word in the sense it is applied by Mr. Pope:

Attach, to tack or fasten together.

Scene VI. Lear, Gloster, Edgar.

The distraction of Lear, in this progress of the play, is wrought up to the highest pitch of frenzy. The author avails himself of the situation, in which he has placed his principal character, to introduce, from his mouth, some very severe and pointed satire: equal to any that can be read in any ancient or modern writer.

L E A R.

But to the girdle do the gods inherit.

Whether Shakspeare had read Brantome, part of whose works had, I believe, been published before this tragedy was acted, I know not; but that free writer, in his Lives of his amorous old Dames, tells us of an agreeable conversation he once had, with a beautiful and worthy *(honeste)* lady, when he was at the court of Spain. Amongst other choice matter, she observed to him, *Que ningunas damas lindas se hacen viejas de la cinta hasta a baxo*, That no fine women were ever old from the girdle downwards.——The rest of Brantome's conversation with this good lady may possibly entertain the reader; and I shall give it in the Frenchman's own words, which, on account of their naïveté, are, I think, not easily translated:

Sur quoy je luy demanday comment elle l'entendoit ? si c'étoit de la beauté du corps, depuis cette ceinture jusques en bas, qu'elle n'en diminuast par la vielesse; ou pour l'envie et l'appetit de la concupiscence, qui ne vinssent à ne n'esteindre ni à se refroidir aucunement par le bas ?—Elle repondit, qu'elle entendoit et pour l'une et pour l'autre : car, pour ce qui est de la picqueure de la chaire, disoit-elle, ne faut pas penser qu'on se guerisse jusques à la mort, quoique l'usage y veuille répugner.

LEAR.

Draw the curtains.

The author of Rabelais's Life puts these words into his mouth when dying; upon what authority I know not.

EDGAR.

To know our enemies' minds we'd rip their hearts.

To put enemies to the rack, to extort confession, is surely not the meaning of the generous Edgar, as Dr. Warburton supposes. The probable intention of the author is, ' If, to acquire the knowledge of our enemies' intentions against us, we put in practice every allowable act, it surely can be no breach of good manners to unseal and read their letters !'

IDEM.

O undistinguish'd space of woman's will !

Dr. Warburton indulges himself with some severe satire against the fair sex, by an illiberal interpretation of this passage.—But he might have spared Virgil's *Varium et mutabile semper fœmina,*
as

as well as Sancho's arch proverb. Edgar's reflection imports no more, than that a vicious woman sets no bounds to her appetites: such an one he knew Goneril was, and to her it is applied.

Scene VII.

In the progress of Lear's distraction, he is brought, by the poet, into a delirium; and, as the recovery from this situation is one of the most powerful efforts of the great poet's genius, to stop and view a little this most pathetic of all interviews, between a delirious father and his affectionate daughter, will not surely be called an ostentatious parade of words or a feeble effort at panegyric. That, which does so much honour to the English stage, cannot be passed over as the mere effusion of a common mind. One great design of Shakspeare, in the choice of this fable, was to hold forth to mankind the unhappy consequences of yielding to the sudden and impetuous impressions of anger.

To trace the poet, in his moral process.—We see him introduce a character, amiable in many respects, brave, generous, frank, and benevolent; but, at the same time, wilful, rash, violent, and headstrong. One unhappy resolution, owing to the fervour of his disposition, precipitates himself and his dearest friends into inextricable ruin: from the short fury of anger he is provoked, by the cunning of the scene, into unlimited resentment, furious indignation, and the most violent rage. Consequent agony and distress lead him to the door of madness. Reason is at length dethroned, and a high paroxysm of frenzy succeeds. Nature affords some relief by a
deliquium.

deliquium. Repose and medicinal application gently restore reason to her proper seat. Here, then, the interview opens, between the unhappy Father, just returning into sensation, and the pious Daughter watching with impatience for a parent's returning intelligence. How affecting is Cordelia's supplication, when she kisses her sleeping father!

>————————Restoration, hang
> Thy med'cine on my lips; and let this kiss
> Repair those violent harms that my two sisters
> Have in thy reverence made!

I am sorry this most beautiful incident was overlooked in the representation.————When Lear awakes, Shakspeare, forgetting that Lear is a heathen, puts into his mouth the words of one in purgatory:

> Thou art a soul in bliss; but I am bound
> Upon a wheel of fire, that mine own tears
> Do scald like molten lead.

On Cordelia's falling on her knees, and imploring his benediction, Lear kneels to his daughter, not knowing who she was or what he did.

The several breaks and interruptions, of imperfect reason and recovering sense, are superior to all commendation, and breathe the most affecting pathos:

> ———— I am mightily abus'd!
> I should die with pity to see another thus!—
> I fear I am not in my perfect mind.

At

At laſt he recollects his dear Cordelia :

——————— Do not laugh at me :
For, as I am a man, I think that lady
To be my child, Cordelia !

The audience, which had been ſighing at the former part of the ſcene, could not ſuſtain this affecting climax, but broke out into loud lamentations.

Be your tears wet ?

ſays Lear, putting his hand upon the cheeks of Cordelia : as if he had ſaid, Can you really feel grief for one who ſo cruelly treated you ?

I D E M.

——————Yes, faith !

I appeal to all, who are converſant in ancient or modern dramatic poetry, whether this ſcene of domeſtic ſorrow be not ſuperior, in compoſition, to all they ever read ! The Greek tragedians, who deal much in demi-gods, too often raiſe their heroes above humanity. The French either imitate their manner, or make their principal characters too national. Shakſpeare alone draws ſuch men as all nations and all ages will acknowledge to be of kin to them. Cibber and others juſtly lament, that the beauties of elocution and action ſhould die with their poſſeſſors, and cannot, by any art, be tranſmitted to poſterity. They, who have had the exquiſite pleaſure to ſee Mr. Garrick in King Lear, will moſt unfeignedly wiſh that his action and elocution could have been perpetuated. A Reynolds could have faithfully tranſcribed a look and an attitude ; but,
alas !

alas! this would have been but an imperfect representation. The wonders of his voice and multiplied expression could not have been preserved!

In the preceding scenes of Lear, Garrick had displayed all the force of quick transition from one passion to another: he had, from the most violent rage, descended to sedate calmness; had seized, with unutterable sensibility, the various impressions of terror, and faithfully represented all the turbid passions of the soul; he had pursued the progress of agonizing feelings to madness in its several stages. Yet, after he had done all this, he exhibited himself, in this fine scene, in such a superior taste, as to make it more interesting than any thing the audience had already enjoyed. But indeed the incident itself is very striking. --- Every spectator feels for himself and common humanity, when he perceives man, while living, degraded to the deprivation of sense and loss of memory! Who does not rejoice, when the creative hand of the poet, in the great actor, restores him to the use of his faculties!

Mrs Cibber, the most pathetic of all actresses, was the only Cordelia of excellence. The discovery of Lear, in prison, sleeping with his head on her lap, his hand closed in her's, whose expressive look spoke more than the most eloquent language, raised the most sympathising emotions.--- Mrs. Davies, during Mrs. Cibber's illness, was invited to supply her place. She did not pretend to imitate that which was not to be attained by imitation, the action, voice, and manner, of Mrs. Cibber. Mrs. Davies's figure, look, and deportment, were esteemed to be so correspondent

dent with the idea of this amiable character, that she was dismissed with no inconsiderable share of approbation.

Act V. Scene II.

EDGAR.

Draw thy sword.

I fear it is almost useless, at this distance of time, to enquire who played the part of Edgar originally. If I might be indulged a conjecture, upon a matter so uncertain, I should fancy that the characters of Lear and Edgar were given, by the author, to Burbage and Taylor, and that the latter was the Edgar. Though this actor was the original Hamlet, it is generally admitted that Burbage was the first tragic player of the age. Taylor was the Iago to Burbage's and Swanston's Othello. Wilks, for many years, most probably from about 1705 to 1729, (when Lear was discontinued on account of Booth's illness,) pleased the public with his animated representation of Edgar. Till the appearance of Barry, no lover like Wilks, since Mountfort, had stepped upon the English stage. That he acquired possession of the part must have been owing to the irregular conduct of George Powell, who had stronger pretensions of voice, figure, action, and manner, by the confession even of Cibber, who seems to have hated Powell. Smith, on the revival of Lear by Tate, represented Edgar; but, on his death, in 1695, it was given to Powell. Wilks excelled in the scenes of love and gallantry, nor was he deficient in the assumed madness, of Edgar. Ryan, I have reason to believe, from what
I heard

I heard from Roberts, the comedian, copied Powell's manner, whom he had attended to when very young. Not to place Ryan on the same bench with Wilks, for that would be unjust, in the comic scenes of Edgar he displayed considerable skill. In the challenge of Edmund, Wilks was highly spirited, with superior elegance of deportment. Ryan's whole behaviour, in the fight and challenge was manly and feeling. Havard, who acted Edgar many years, had seen these actors in the part, and formed a very pleasing manner from both. Nor must we forget the merit of the unfortunate Reddish; who, in the opinion of the public, and the great manager, his employer, was acknowledged to have well understood and represented the character.

EDGAR.

The gods are just, and from our pleasant vices
Make instruments to scourge us.

Of all dramatic authors, ancient and modern, Shakspeare is the most moral. Dr. Johnson, in his admirable preface to our author, is of opinion, that his frequent moralizing did not proceed from premeditated intention or design. I should imagine, that it must have formed one part of his general plan in the writing of his dramas, otherwise he could not have so frequently adopted that mode of writing; any more than a clergyman could, by chance, perpetually preach on moral, and never on positive duties.

EDMUND.

EDMUND.

This speech of yours hath mov'd me.

The obdurate and cruel Edmund feels no tenderness and remorse, till roused by the relation of his father's death, pathetically described by Edgar. This is finely touched, as well as artfully contrived, by the author; for it introduces the notice of Lear and Cordelia, for whom the audience must have been in pain.

Walker, the original Macheath, acted Edmund with a vigour and spirit which were only below his personating the Bastard Falconbridge, in King John, on account of the inferiority of one character to another. When he spoke the first soliloquy, " Thou, Nature, art my goddess ! &c." the audience justified the selecting him for the daring and intrepid part. Walker's action, which was taught him by Booth, was extremely easy and natural: his tread was manly, and his whole behaviour and deportment disengaged and commanding. I cannot, with equal praise, speak of any other Edmund in Lear.

Scene X. and last.

[*Lear brings in the dead Cordelia in his arms.*]

KENT.

Is this the promis'd end ?

" Do all my hopes of Lear's restoration end in his distraction and the death of Cordelia?"

EDGAR.

EDGAR.

Or image of that horror!

" Is it not rather a scene of the most unspeakable horror?"

ALBANY.

Fall and cease.

Perhaps Albany means, " lower your voice, and cease all exclamation, lest you interrupt the dying King." This is not unlike, in sense, to the word *quietness* in Antony and Cleopatra: Charmion, on the Queen's fainting, whispers to Iras, *O quietness!*

Successive audiences, by their persevering approbation, have justified the happy ending of this tragedy, with the restoration of Lear and the marriage of Cordelia and Edgar.

Tho' Tate's alterations are, in many places mean and unworthy to be placed so near the composition of the best dramatic author, it must be confessed, that in the conduct of some scenes, whether contrived by himself, or hinted to him by his friend Dryden, he is not unhappy. One situation of his is particularly affecting: where the scene opens, and discovers Lear, with his head on Cordelia's lap, and the King in his sleep, attacking the forces of his enemies. The bringing that action forward to the audience, which is only related in the old play, of Lear's killing the two soldiers employed to murder him and Cordelia, is a circumstance that gives pleasure and exultation to the spectators. The half breathing and panting of Garrick, with a look and action which con-

confessed the infirmity of old age, greatly heightened the picture. To speak in Shakspeare's phrase, this incident will be *locked in the memory* of those who have the pleasure to remember it. Barry, in this scene, was a lively copy of Garrick's manner, and had the superior advantage of a more important figure. Who could possibly think of depriving an audience, almost exhausted with the feelings of so many terrible scenes, of the inexpressible delight which they enjoyed, when the old King, in rapture, cried out——

Old Lear shall be a king again!

In this last, and the foregoing speech of Lear, Booth was inimitably expressive, from the full tones of his voice, and the admirable manner of harmonizing his words. Upon the whole, Booth rendered the character of Lear more amiable, or, to speak critically, less terrible, than Garrick.—— The latter went more deeply into his author's meaning; and expressed the various passions of the character with such truth and energy, that no audience ever saw him without astonishment as well as rapture. There was a particular compliment paid to the exhibition of this tragedy, beyond all others. After a very loud plaudit at the end of the play, when the curtain was let fall, the spectators testified their complete pleasure and satisfaction, by renewing their loud applauses two or three several times.——Lear was, in the opinion of a great number of the best judges, Mr. Garrick's masterpiece. When this inimitable actor was buried, a person, it is said, by desire of Mrs. Garrick, threw the play of Hamlet into the grave with the corpse. With equal,

equal, if not more, propriety, Lear might have also been deposited there.

Amongst a number of Shakspeare's capital plays, it is not easy to determine in which the genius of the writer shone out with greatest lustre. However, I believe it will be confessed, that in none of his tragedies the passions have been extended with more genuine force, the incidents more numerous or more dramatically conducted, nor the moral more profitable, than in Lear. There are three characters, in this play, of which I scarcely know that there are any counterparts in any other, ancient or modern. They are, indeed, all martyrs to virtue and piety. Though too much cannot be said of the generous offspring of our inimitable bard, Kent can no where be matched. Edgar and Cordelia follow next: such an example as Cordelia, of filial piety, except perhaps in the Grecian stage, * is not to be found in dramatic poetry. Edgar is equal in merit to the lady.

I shall conclude my observations on this tragedy with a theatrical anecdote.

Amongst the actresses who personated Cordelia, when Boheme acted Lear, there was a young woman whose name was Stone. Her history is so singular, that I think it merits a place in this Miscellany.

Miss Stone's genteel figure, agreeable countenance, and pleasing voice, recommended her to the notice of Mr. Rich; who, about the year 1725, employed her to act in his theatre of Lincoln's-

---

* The Antigone of Sophocles, in the OEdipus Colonæus, is a most perfect character of filial piety.

coln's-inn Fields. The unaffected and elegant manner she displayed in a variety of parts, chiefly such as attract our notice from youth, modesty, and gentleness, pleased the public. Mr. C———, a young gentleman, heir to a large estate, fell passionately in love with her.———As he could not obtain her consent to his addresses, without the matrimonial bond, the warmth of his passion impelled him to marry her. The father no sooner heard of this indiscreet and disproportioned match, than he commanded his son to return home to the family seat, which was not many miles distant from the metropolis. The son, through dread of his father's displeasure, obeyed; and the new-married pair were parted, never to meet again.

The family, shocked at the unequal match, determined, at all events, to bring about a separation. In order to carry on their design, they prevailed on the manager of the playhouse, by intimidation or other means, never to suffer Mrs. C. to act upon his stage. The next step was to prove the wife's incontinency; and, to this end, they addressed themselves to a gay man of fashion, who was base enough to engage in their conspiracy. This man made his addresses to Mrs. C. with a view to debauch her. The poor unhappy young woman, being separated from her husband, by fraudulent and oppressive arts deprived of the means of gaining a maintenance from the theatre, and surrounded with poverty, fell a prey to the insidious attempts of a man who had held out to her the means of present relief. The gentleman had no sooner accomplished his ends than he forsook her. She soon after perished in great affliction and distress. Whether the husband
be

be still living I know not. The man of fashion became afterwards an eminent writer; I hope he sincerely repented the shameful part he acted in this iniquitous transaction.

Antony

Antony and Cleopatra.

CHAP. XXXIII.

Ben Jonson's ridicule on Shakspeare's Antony and Cleopatra.—Dr. Johnson's opinion of that tragedy.—May's Cleopatra.—Dryden's All for Love.—Sir Charles Sedley.—Fulvia's character.—Epigram of Augustus.—Tears of an onion.—Mr. Steevens mistaken.—Arm-gaunt steed explained.—Cleopatra's sallad days.—Several other passages interpreted.—K. Charles I. and Mr. Hyde.—Antony's bounty.—Quick comedians.—The custom of ridiculing all characters on the Athenian stage.—Lord-mayor of London and Lord Burleigh.—Custom of boys acting women's parts.—Shakspeare's female characters.—Who was the first actress that appeared on the London stage.—French actresses.—Spanish theatre.—Baretti's account of it—The pope suffers none but eunuchs to play in operas.—Countryman and aspic.—Cleopatra's noble preparation for death.—Whether killed by poison or the aspic.—Her character.—Dr. Johnson's criticism examined.—Garrick and Mrs. Yates.—Dryden's All for Love.—Booth and Oldfield.—Mills.—Wilks.—Colley Cibber.—Mrs. Porter.

Ben Jonson, in his Silent Woman, has apparently, though obliquely, treated this tragedy as a play full of nothing but empty noise and fights by sea, with drum, trumpet, and target; nor does Dr. Johnson, I think, rank it amongst those of our author's dramas which are greatly esteemed. Yet of all the plays written on the subject of Antony and Cleopatra, this most interests the passions, and consequently is most dramatic. It represents more of action, character, and manners, than May's Cleopatra or Dryden's All for Love. As to the Antony and Cleopatra of Sir Charles Sedley, it was lucky for the author, that he wrote some years after the Rehearsal had been acted; or, in all probability, he would have made no inconsiderable figure in that comic satire.

It is true that there are not, in Shakspeare's Antony and Cleopatra, as in many of our author's pieces, many striking and important scenes. According to his plan, of crouding the greatest part of Antony's life, from the death of Fulvia till he killed himself in Alexandria, that would not have been possible.

The minutiæ of events described lessen the grandeur of the whole. The several pictures are, in themselves, however, compleat, and give great variety and entertainment; though it was impossible they should be all of them, either finely coloured or highly finished. There is, in this play, perhaps, more of that general character by which Pope distinguishes our author from other great writers: " The genius of Shakspeare
strikes

strikes ere we are aware, like an accidental fire from heaven." The two principal characters are as wild and irregular in the scene as they were in their lives.

Sir Charles Sedley could either have no veneration for Shakſpeare, or had great confidence in his own abilities. He has borrowed very little from him, and has ſpoiled what he took. Dryden, on the contrary, ſeems to have been, in many ſcenes of his All for Love, inſpired with the warm flame of the original. In endeavouring to imitate his maſter, he has excelled himſelf. Ventidius is a ſober Enobarbus. Antony, in the firſt act, is ſo great, that the poet wanted power to keep pace with himſelf, and falls off from his firſt ſetting out. Dryden's Cleopatra has none of the various feminine artifices, and ſhapes of paſſions, of the original; nor, indeed that greatneſs of ſoul which ennobles her laſt ſcenes in Shakſpeare. She reſembles more the artful kept-miſtreſs, than the irregular, but accompliſhed, Queen of Egypt.

Act I. Scene I.

CLEOPATRA.

When ſhrill-tongu'd Fulvia ſcolds.

Fulvia, ſucceſſively the wife of Clodius, Curio, and Mark Antony, was a moſt extraordinary woman. She ſcorned all domeſtic employment; not content with governing her huſbands at home, ſhe aſpired to rule over them in public, in the cabinet and the field, to direct their counſels, and to command their troops. She had, for a long time, an abſolute power over Antony; whom she tamed so thoroughly, by the vigor of her spirit, that she left no work of that sort for Cleopatra. Cicero, in one of his Philippics, intimates, that he conceived great hopes of Antony's ruin from his connection with that turbulent woman. Rome, said the orator, had already received two payments from her, meaning the deaths of Clodius and Curio; and was in expectation of a third, by the speedy destruction of Antony. To this severe sarcasm we may perhaps attribute the shocking behaviour of this virago to the head of Cicero, when brought to her. With bitter upbraidings she placed it in her lap; she first extracted the tongue from the head; and afterwards, with the bodkin, pricked it several times, still uttering the most poignant and abusive expressions.† It is generally said, that her jealousy of Cleopatra excited her to make war upon Octavius. However, if we may believe the epigram, in Martial, attributed to Augustus, he might, if he pleased, have accommodated the matter upon easier terms than fighting. The spirit of this piece of wit consists in Fulvia's offering Octavius a share in her bed, or else threatening a struggle for conquest in the field. 'If that be the case,' the triumvir cried, ' sound trumpets and beat drums, for any thing is preferable to this lady's favours.' This high-spirited dame was at last conquered by her husband's neglect and reproaches. He severely chid her, by letter, for raising disturbances in Italy. She died at Sicyon, on the road to Athens; and this event accelerated a match between the amiable Octavia and Mark Antony.

Scene

† Dion Cassius.

Scene II.

CHARMION.

Nay, if an oily palm be not a fruitful prognostication, I cannot scratch my ear.

This is similar to a passage in Othello, act III. where Othello, jealous of his wife, takes her by the hand:

> This hand of your's is moist, my lady.

―――――

> There is a young and sweating devil here,
> That commonly rebels.

ENOBARBUS.

And, indeed, the tears live in an onion that should water this sorrow.

That is, 'Fulvia's death will cause no real grief in you; the tears, which you will shed on this occasion, resemble such as are extracted by the application of an onion to the eye. *If you cannot cry, clap an onion to your eye,* has been, I believe, an old sarcasm on forced sorrow. Suidas records a Greek proverb, which proves the power of an onion to draw tears: Κρομμυα ισθιιν, *Cepas edere:* and he quotes, from a lost comedy of Aristophanes, Κρομμυα τ'αρ υκ εδη, αντι, υκ εκλαι, *Cepas non comedit,* for *non flevit.*—Mr. Steevens has not, I think, understood the passage: an onion has, certainly, in contradiction to what he asserts, much moisture in it.

CLEOPATRA.

Though you in swearing shake the throned gods.

So, in Timon, *And to strong shudders swear th'
immortal gods.*

ANTONY.

─────But my full heart
Remains in use to you.

' I leave my heart with you as a pledge that I
will never forsake you.'

Scene V. Cleopatra, Iras, &c.

ALEXAS.

And soberly did mount an *arm-gaunt steed.*

Much has been said about the meaning of
arm-gaunt steed. In ridicule, I suppose, of Warburton's explanation, Mr. Edwards compared
the horse, that bore the great master of a third
part of the globe, to the lean and emaciated Rosinante of Don Quixote. Dr. Johnson would suppose him to be a post-horse; as if Antony were
reduced to the necessity of taking up with such
horses as were to be found at an inn upon the
road. I think the Emperor might, at least, be
allowed the same liberty which Jack Falstaff assumed, when he heard his old friend and companion, Prince Hal, was king: *The laws of England are at my command; let us take any man's
horses!* We may reasonably suppose, that the
horse which bore Mark Antony, was remarkable
for size and beauty. The Romans were particularly

cularly attentive to the breed, as well as management, of horses. *Arm-gaunt* means *fine-shaped*, or *thin-shouldered*. *I must suppose*, says Bracken, *that every one is sensible that thin-shouldered horses move the best.*—*Arm gaunt*, I think, is a word compounded of the Latin word, *armus*, and *gaunt*: the latter is an old word well known, and *armus*, a shoulder, originally signified that part of a man's body, but the Latin writers afterwards more frequently applied it to the animal.

CLEOPATRA.

——————— My *sallad days*,
When I was green in judgment, cold in blood.

The Queen talks like a woman well experienced in love-matters. Her commerce with Cæsar commenced when she was young, and he was advanced to the fifty-fourth year of his age. Mark Antony was in the warm summer of life when he first beheld this wonder of attraction, having not seen more than thirty-three or thirty-four years. In comparing her two lovers, Cleopatra may well be justified in calling her first passion, 'the effects of her *sallad-days*, greenness of judgment and coolness of blood.'

Scene IV.

LEPIDUS.

His faults in him seem as the spots of heav'n,
More fiery by night's blackness.

Exactness of expression must not be expected from a writer who takes up with the first words that come in his way. It is very plain, that

L 3 Shak-

Shakspeare, by the night's blackness, meant only the absence of the sun. The stars shine brightest when the blaze of day is absent.

OCTAVIUS.

———————— Say this becomes him,
(As his composition must be rare indeed,
Whom these things cannot blemish.)

I cannot think, with Dr. Johnson, that Cæsar's argument is inconsequent. It is a very common mode of expression to say, that " such a person is guilty of many absurdities, which his friends will say, perhaps, become him; and suppose I should grant all this, though he must be a very extraordinary man indeed if they do, yet, &c." The parenthesis does not hurt the logical conclusion of the main proposition. Dr. Johnson's reading is a very good explanation of the text.

Scene V.

CLEOPATRA.

——————And great Pompey
Would stand, and make his eyes grow in my brow;
There would he anchor his aspect, and die
With looking on his life.

This is finely imitated, by Southern, in a beautiful apostrophe to Imoinda by the tender and passionate Oroonoko:

My soul steals from my body through my eyes;
All that is left of life I'll *gaze away*,
And die upon the pleasure!

The

The image is also copied by the learned and elegant Fenton, in his Marianne, tho' not so warmly, yet in conformity to the object and occasion.

Marianne, taking leave of her beloved infant, just going to be made a hostage at Rome, among other tender sentiments, breaks out into the following:

> No more must these desiring eyes be fix'd
> In silent joy with gazing on thy charms!

Act II. Scene II.

Octavius, Antony, Lepidus, &c.

CÆSAR.

Sit.

ANTONY.

Sit, sir.

CÆSAR.

Nay, then;

Mr. Steevens is of opinion, that Antony is offended at the assumed superiority of Cæsar, in bidding him sit who was his equal. Can we suppose that Antony would come from Egypt to renew his friendship with Octavius, and take umbrage at a mere matter of form? Nothing passes between the triumvirs but what every body would expect. One politely invites the other to take his seat. The other returns the civility. Octavius puts an end to the ceremony, by saying, *Nay, then*, that is, 'Let us not protract time by needless form.' Antony, during the whole scene,

scene, is modest and temperate; and is rather the apologist than vindicator of his past conduct.

ENOBARBUS.

————— Your considerate stone.

Αγιλαστος πιτρα, *the unlaughing stone*, is an old Greek proverb; and *As dumb or dead as a stone* is familiar, I should think, to most languages. Mr. Steevens's conceit of the marble statue is more ingenious than solid.

ANTONY.

I did not think to draw my sword 'gainst Pompey;
For he hath laid strange courtesies and great
Of late upon me. I must thank him only
Lest my remembrance suffer ill report :
At heel of that, defy him.

Dr. Johnson says, on this passage, that Antony unwilling to be thought forgetful of benefits, says, 'I must barely return him thanks, and then defy him.' This cannot, I think, be Shakspeare's intention. One man receives great and unexpected favours from another. How does he repay them? by barely returning thanks to the kind donor, and then hurling defiance in his teeth! More is surely understood: 'Let me first,' says Antony, 'return the obligation I owe Pompey in such a manner as becomes me; and then I shall think myself at liberty to join with you in declaring war against him.'

Scene II.

CLEOPATRA.

O that his fault should make a knave of thee,
That art not what thou art sure of!

These lines have much perplexed the commentators. But a small alteration in the pointing, and the addition of a single letter, will remove all difficulties.

Cleopatra cannot endure to hear of Antony's marriage; and, notwithstanding the Messenger perseveres in telling her the same story, she persists in asking repeatedly whether he is married or not: at last, as if she had been sated with disagreeable confirmations of what she wished not to believe, she laments that Antony's crime should make the Messenger dishonest, who in reality was not so. But the odious marriage still haunting her memory, before she dismisses him she adds, 'What! thou art sure of it!' that is, 'He is certainly married!' The Messenger, we may suppose, confirms by action what he had so often affirmed in words; and she then dismisses him. The lines, then, with this trifling alteration, will read thus:

O that his fault should make a knave of thee,
That art not!—What! thou'rt sure of't!—Get thee hence!

Scene III.

CÆSAR.

Will this satisfy him?

ANTONY.

With the health that Pompey gives him, else he is a very epicure.

Antony's answer is ironical: 'Lepidus, with the help of wine, will take up with this solution of his question: but, when he is sober, his judgment is so strong, that he is a perfect epicure in the art of doubting.'

ENOBARBUS.

[ON SEEING LEPIDUS CARRIED OFF DRUNK.]

There's a strong fellow, Menas.

MENAS.

————Why?

ENOBARBUS.

————He bears
The third part of the world, man; seest not?

MENAS.

The third part, then, is drunk.

As Lord Chesterfield was going from the rooms at Bath to his apartments, he saw somebody carried home drunk in a chair. He asked who it was? 'Quin, my lord, going home from the three Tuns.'————'That is a mistake, sir,' replied his lordship, 'for he has carried one of the three tuns home in his belly.'

Act III. Scene V.

CLEOPATRA.

What shall we do, Enobarbus?

ENOBARBUS.

ENOBARBUS.

————*Think and die.*

Hanmer has proposed *Drink and die,* and brings Plutarch's story of a social club to support his reading. Had Enobarbus been asked this question at a feast, or a drinking-bout, the answer would have been in character: but, to a serious question, proposed to an eminent soldier by a queen, such a reply would have been improper, and indeed brutal, nor would his character of humour have excused it. Besides, his answer to the next question, put to him by Cleopatra, ' Whether she or Antony was in fault?' without any farther examination, confirms the reading as preserved by the last editors.

ENOBARBUS.

————And be staged to the show
Against a sworder.

' ————Fight with him like a gladiator upon a stage, for the diversion of the populace.'

ANTONY.

But, when we in our viciousness grow hard,
O mis'ry on't! the wife gods seal our eyes.

This alludes to that doctrine which tells us,— when we become irreclaimable in our vices, heaven judicially blinds us.

IDEM.

————Nay, you were a fragment
Of Cneius Pompey's.

Not

Not Pompey the Great as Mr. Tollet imagines, but his eldest son, Cneius.

IDEM.

Let a fellow that will take rewards.

That is, 'Suffer a poor menial servant to be familiar with you, whose condition in life subjects him to the meanness of taking vails, or small presents, for officious attendance.'

Would you flatter one who *ties his points?*

Tying of points, in our author's time, was the office of a menial servant, or, as we now say, a valet de chambre: hence, metaphorically, it signifies a low and servile office. When Mr. Hyde, afterwards Earl of Clarendon, some time before the beginning of the civil wars, waited upon Charles I. at Hampton-court, the king said to him, 'So, Ned Hyde, *they say you tie my points!*'

IDEM.

————————When my hours were *nice* and lucky.

The word *nice* has many significations in Shakspeare and other old English writers. Here Antony certainly means, 'When my time was spent in pleasure, gaiety, and happiness.'

IDEM.

Let's mock the midnight bell.

The pleasures of revelling all night, and extending them to the morning, are often mentioned with glee by our author; but no where more

more pleasantly than when noted by Falstaff, who calls a midnight debauch *the sweet morsel of the night*.

IDEM.

—————The next time I do fight,
I will make death love me; for I will contend
Ev'n with his pestilent scythe.

Something very like the two first half-lines we find in Measure for Measure, spoken by Claudio to Isabella:

—————If I must die,
I will encounter darkness as a bride,
And hug it in my arms.

Dryden, in his All for Love, act I. has nobly extended the whole passage, and more especially the latter part of the quotation:

—————I long
Once more to meet our foes; that thou and I,
Like time and death, marching before our troops,
May taste fate to them; mow them out a passage;
And, ent'ring where the foremost squadrons yield,
Begin the noble *harvest* of the field.

Act IV. Scene II.

ANTONY.

—————Oh! my fortunes have
Corrupted honest men!

Amidst all the folly, profligacy, and mad flights, of Mark Antony, some bright beams of a great and generous soul break forth with inimitable lustre. Instead of reproaching his officer for desertion and treachery, he lays the blame on his now adverse fortune, which had unhappily overthrown

thrown the principles of the best and worthiest men. This is one of our author's characteristical strokes, and perfectly suited to Mark Antony.

SOLDIER.

[AFTER DELIVERING TO ENOBARBUS HIS TREASURE.]

——————Your emperor
Continues still a Jove.

The bounty of Antony went hand in hand with his rapacity. As he omitted no means, however unjust, to acquire wealth, so he was equally liberal in bestowing it. A lively sentiment, or a smart repartee, would sometimes recal him from the commission of flagrant acts of injustice, though nothing could stop the floodgates of his generosity. When he had resolved to exact double taxes from the greatest part of Asia, he was told, if he persisted in his determination, he must also give that part of the world double seasons, two winters and two summers in the year. This pertinent reproof prevented him from committing a cruel act of oppression. To a person, whom he much befriended, he ordered his steward to give a very large sum of money. The man thought the gift so exorbitant, that, to excite his caution and convince him of his prodigality, he spread the money, in large heaps, upon several tables. The emperor, understanding the intention of the steward, and scorning to retract his order, said, very coolly, ' that he thought the sum of money had been much greater;' and commanded him to give his friend double the quantity.

SOLDIER.

SOLDIER.

We will purfue them into bench-holes.

'We will purfue them, with blows, till we force them to feek for shelter under tables and benches.'

ANTONY.

Would'ft thou be window'd in great Rome?

'Would'ft thou be gazed at from *windows* and tops of houfes in the ftreets of Rome?'

IDEM.

Pleach'd arms.

Arms tied behind him, as captives were obliged to walk after the victor's triumphal chariot.

EROS, [KILLING HIMSELF.]

—There, then! thus do I efcape the forrow
Of Antony's death!

Eros generoufly killing himfelf, rather than be the inftrument to murder his Emperor, is copied, with great judgment, by Dryden, in his All for Love, who has made a proper diftinction between an old brother-officer and a freedman. Eros modeftly begs from his mafter a parting farewell: Ventidius claims a laft embrace, as from a friend. The paffage deferves to be quoted:

VENTIDIUS.

VENTIDIUS.

——————Give me your hand;
We soon shall meet again. Now farewel, emperor!
Methinks that word's too cold to be my last,
Since death sweeps all distinction : farewel, friend!

Act V. Scene I.

CÆSAR.

——————He *mocks*:
The pauses which he makes.

' By these wretched delays, he does but expose his conduct to derision.' *Mock* is a favourite word with Shakspeare, and applied by him variously, but generally to vain and impotent endeavours.

IDEM.

——————Hear me, good friends.——
But I will tell you at some meeter season.

So, in Julius Cæsar, Brutus, lamenting over the dead body of Cassius,——

Cassius, I shall find time, I shall find time !

Scene II.

PROCULEIUS.

——————You shall find
A conqueror that will pray in aid for kindness.

That is, ' he will himself turn solicitor for you.'

IDEM.

IDEM.

[AFTER PREVENTING CLEOPATRA FROM STABBING HERSELF.]

―――――Hold, worthy lady, hold;
Do not yourself such wrong, who are in this
Reliev'd, but not betray'd.

There is no necessity to alter the word *relieved* for *bereaved*, or any other word. *Relieved* alludes to a town besieged, which, by the sudden arrival of social forces, is freed from the besiegers.

CLEOPATRA.

This is the *brief* of money, &c.

' This is the *inventory*.'

IDEM.

Parcel the sum of my disgrace.

That is, adding another item to the gross sum of her misfortunes, by her steward's ingratitude.

IDEM.

―――――The quick comedians
Extemporally will stage us.

Whether the comedians of Rome laid hold of every public matter, and turned it into a subject for stage-exhibition, is not, I believe, very certain. That the English comedians often bring on the stage, for their emolument, public, and sometimes private, transactions, cannot be controverted. Let the Receipt-tax, a farce, be an instance. But, in such matters, the Athenians excelled all mankind; for they, without distinction, brought upon their theatre all facts, faults,

and

and blemishes, whatsoever. The old comedy exhibited, in person, the best as well as the worst of the Athenian citizens, just as the malignity or humour of the author prompted. In their inferior dramatic pieces, the smallest defects of their demagogues, or public orators, were imitated and ridiculed. Any distinguished pleasantry of any man of note was sure to be laid hold of by the Athenian players, and exposed to public view. Nor is there a more common expression, in some of the old Greek critics, particularly the scholiast of Aristophanes, than that such an one was brought upon the stage for some peculiarity or other in his gait, dress, look, manner of living; for his pride, extravagance, luxury, &c.

Something of this all stages have had in their original state. When some great lords complained, to Louis XII. of France, that the comedians made free with his majesty and the court, 'I am glad of it,' said that good prince, 'for I shall be sure to hear the truth;' and immediately gave orders that the comedians should play before him, and desired them to spare nobody. But this worthy king's good-nature is no excuse for the licentiousness of his players.—' The stage,' says honest Dodsley, in his preface to his edition of old English plays, ' no sooner learned to speak, than it grew scurrilous, and a chief magistrate of London complained, that Lord Burleigh had encouraged the common players to represent his father on their stage.'

C L E O P A T R A.

―――――――――And I shall see
Some squeaking Cleopatra *boy* my greatness.

This

This refers to the custom, in Shakspeare's time, of boys, or young and handsome lads, acting women's parts. Our author sometimes takes notice of the diminutive size of these boy-ladies. In Twelfth Night, Sir Toby Belch calls his niece's woman, 'the youngest of nine wrens.'—Some critics have supposed, that the female characters of Shakspeare are not drawn with equal force and spirit, nor with that elegance and delicacy, as in other writers, on account of having such improper representatives. But I believe it will be difficult to find, in any author, such abundant and varied originality, in women's characters, as in Shakspeare.* The ladies indeed, of Beaumont and Fletcher, are, in general, of a different complexion; few of them are marked with simplicity, elegance, modesty, and sensibility; for the most part they are of the virago kind, bold, licentious, and violent, fitted, for the tomboys who acted them. Aspasia in the Maid's Tragedy, Juliana in the Double Marriage, Lucina in Valentinian, and a few more, are sweet exceptions.——Charles II. put an end to the ridiculous and absurd custom of men acting women's parts. A number of beautiful actresses soon gave a new lustre to the English theatre. The first woman-actress was the mother of Norris, commonly called Jubilee Dicky.——The French stage was, I believe, sooner enlivened with women than the English, though they could boast of nothing but poor imitations of the ancients,

---

* Cleopatra, Juliet, Imogen, Ophelia, Lady Constance, Isabella, Volumnia, Lady Macbeth, Portia in the Merchant of Venice, Rosalind, Beatrice, are all distinct characters. To these many others might be added.

cients, till the days of Rotrou and Corneille. Baretti, in his Letters from Spain, acquaints us, that, till within these twenty years, all the parts in Spanish plays were acted by women.* The Pope permits none but men or eunuchs to play in the operas at Rome during the carnival.

CLOWN.

I know that a woman is a dish for the gods if the devil dress her not.

Shakspeare well knew the taste of a London audience. The severity of the tragic scenes always wanted some comic relief; he has therefore brought in aid his constant friend, the joker, in the shape of a simple countryman.

CLEOPATRA.

———Methinks I hear
Antony call; I see him rouse himself,
To praise my noble act!

Cleopatra's preparation for death is animated to a degree of sublimity which greatly raises the character of the Egyptian princess, and makes us lament her in death whom living we could not praise, though it was impossible not to admire her.

It has been questioned, by some historians, whether Cleopatra was killed by drinking poison, which she always carried about her, or by the bite of the aspic. Augustus confirms the latter account, by having her figure drawn with an aspic on her arm, and exposed to public view, when he triumphed over Antony.

* Vide the next chapter.

The

ANTONY AND CLEOPATRA.

* The beauty of Cleopatra was not very astonishing; she did not, in feature, surpass many of her sex: but the power of her wit greatly elevated her charms; her manner, too, was enchanting and irresistible. No female could boast of such a voice; for, so great was its variety of modulation, that it resembled an instrument of many strings. She is said to have spoken about thirty languages; there were few foreign ambassadors to whom she could not give audience in their own tongue.

I cannot help thinking that Dr. Johnson has been rather precipitate in deciding upon the merit of Antony and Cleopatra.—How can I submit to that sentence, which pronounces, that there is no discrimination of character, in this play, except in Cleopatra, whom he considers only as conspicuous for feminine arts? Those she has in abundance, it is true; but her generous resolution, to die rather than submit to embrace life upon ignoble terms, is surely also worth remembering. But is not Antony highly discriminated by variety of passion, by boundless generosity, as well as unexampled dotage? What does this truly great writer think of Enobarbus, the rough old warrior, shrewd in his remarks and humorous in his plain-dealing? I shall say nothing of Octavius or Lepidus, though they are certainly separated from other parts. The simplicity of the fable is necessarily destroyed by exhibiting such a croud of events, happening in distant periods of time, a fault common to historical plays. But, in spight of all irregularities, this tragedy remains unequalled by any that have been written on the same subject.

* Plutarch.

Antony and Cleopatra had long lain dormant, I believe ever since it was first exhibited, when, about the year 1760, Mr. Garrick, from his passionate desire to give the public as much of their admired poet as possible, revived it, as altered by Mr. Capel, with all the advantages of new scenes, habits, and other decorations proper to the play. However, it did not answer his own and the public expectation. It must be confessed, that, in Antony, he wanted one necessary accomplishment: his person was not sufficiently important and commanding to represent the part. There is more dignity of action than variety of passion in the character, though it is not deficient in the latter. The actor who is obliged continually to traverse the stage, should from person attract respect, as well as from the power of speech. Mrs. Yates was then a young actress, and had not manifested such proofs of genius, and such admirable elocution, as she has since displayed; but her fine figure and pleasing manner of speaking were well adapted to the enchanting Cleopatra. Mossop wanted the essential part of Enobarbus, humour.

In Dryden's All for Love, Booth's dignified action and forcible elocution, in the part, of Antony, attracted the public to that heavy, tho' in many parts, well-written, play, six nights successively, without the assistance of pantomime or farce, which, at that time was esteemed something extraordinary. But indeed he was well supported by an Oldfield, in his Cleopatra, who, to a most harmonious and powerful voice, and fine person, added grace and elegance of gesture. When Booth and Oldfield met in the second act, their dignity of deportment commanded the applause plaufe and approbation of the moft judicious critics. When Antony faid to Cleopatra,

> You promis'd me your filence, and you break it
> Ere I have fcarce begun,

this check was fo well underftood by Oldfield, and anfwered with fuch propriety of behaviour, that, in Shakfpeare's phrafe, *Her bendings were adornings.*

The elder Mills acted Ventidius with the true fpirit of a rough and generous old foldier. To render the play as acceptable to the public as poffible, Wilks took the trifling part of Dolabella, nor did Colley Cibber difdain to appear in Alexas: thefe parts would fcarcely be accepted now by third-rate actors. Still to add more weight to the performance, Octavia was a fhort character of a fcene or two, in which Mrs. Porter drew not only refpect, but the more affecting approbation of tears, from the audience. Since that time, All for Love has gradually funk into oblivion.

Rule

Rule a Wife and have a Wife.

CHAP. XXXIV.

Plots of Beaumont and Fletcher taken from Spanish novels, and probably from Spanish plays.—Plot of Rule a Wife and have a Wife.—Character of an epicure from Paulus Jovius.—Number of plays by Lope de la Vega.—Cervantes's account of the Spanish theatre.—Spanish Roscius, Lope de Rueda his merit as an actor and writer.—Successor of Rueda.—Plays of Cervantes.—An opposer of Lope de la Vega.—A description of De Vega's uncommon genius.—Calderone, his successor;—debauches the public taste.—Remarkable passages in the life of De Vega.—His marriage and duel.—Secretary to Alva.—Soldier on board the Spanish armada.— Second marriage.—His misfortunes.—Ordained priest.—Honoured with a degree by Pope Urban. —His death and magnificent funeral.—Gazed at when walking the streets.—His great riches.— Works.—Quickness in composition.—His reasons for breaking through the rules of the drama.—His extensive benevolence and charity.—Chances and Rule a Wife, &c.—Garrick incited by Mr. Colman to revive plays of Beaumont and Fletcher and Massinger.—Revival of Philaster and Bonduca. —Powell and Mrs. Yates.—Mr. Colman's edition of Beaumont and Fletcher.—Comedians obliged to Mr. Colman.—How.—Æschylus, Sophocles, Plautus, Terence, Shakspeare, and Moliere.— First play of Shakspeare.—His style imitated by Beaumont

RULE A WIFE AND HAVE A WIFE. 243

Beaumont and Fletcher.—Their composition described.—Reason why the dialogue of Beaumont and Fletcher is generally more polished than Shakspeare's. —Mercutio.—Benedick.—Rosalind.—Prince of Wales and Falstaff.—Licentious style of Beaumont and Fletcher.—Shakspeare, compared to them, modest.—The Captain.—Scornful Lady and Custom of the Country.—Shakspeare's power over his auditors.—Merchant of Venice.—Charles Macklin.— Wife for a Month.—Its plot and manners described at large.—Valerio and Evanthe.—Marriage Bed. —Lelia and her father.—Real excellences of Beaumont and Fletcher flourish for ever.—Shakspeare one of the audience.—Dramatic effect.— Faithful Shepherdess.—Two noble Kinsmen.— Beaumont and Fletcher enviers of Shakspeare.— Rule a Wife and have a Wife acted by Hart and Mohun, &c.—The merit of the play.—Perez, a military coxcomb.—Cacafogo, a bastard Falstaff.— Elder Mills, Wilks, Booth, Mrs. Oldfield.— —Ryan, Mrs. Younger.---Mossop desires to act Leon.—Opposed by Garrick.---Woodward.---Mrs. Cibber, in comedy, misplaced.—Mrs. Clive, Mrs. Pritchard, Mrs. Abington, and Mr. King. —Garrick's great skill in Leon.---The word feeling *explained.*

S E V E R A L plots of Beaumont and Fletcher's plays are taken from Spanish novels, and, in all probability, from Spanish plays. To the first we owe the Chances, Love's Pilgrimage, and Rule a Wife and have a Wife, which are all taken from Cervantes. The last is formed entirely from the *Casamiento enganioso* of this celebrated writer. I am not sufficiently read in the

VOL. II. M theatre

theatre of Spain to point out the originals whence our authors might have borrowed fables, scenes, or characters. As they were very conversant with modern as well as antient literature, we cannot suppose them unacquainted with the plays of Cervantes, or of that voluminous author, distinguished by the glorious title of the *Spanish Shakspeare*, Lope de la Vega. That these celebrated twin-writers were very assiduous in the search of an extraordinary character can be proved, from their having read Paul Jovius de Piscibus Romanis, and taken the whole character of Lazarillo, the nice feeder, from that author; who has, in very classical Latin, given at large the character of a parasite and smell-feast, who, in search of an unbrana, after many disappointments, sat down at table with a courtezan, to enjoy his beloved fish. If the reader should desire to come at this proof of their indefatigable diligence, without consulting P. Jovius de Piscibus Romanis, which is, I believe, not very common, he may turn to the article Chigi in Bayle's Dictionary.

The plays, said to be written by Lope de Vega, amount to the incredible number of 1800; all which were acted, and the greatest part of them with applause. Lope may be truly said, like Pope, to have *lisped in numbers*, for he began to make verses before he had learned to write. He bribed his elder schoolfellows, with a part of his breakfast, to commit to paper the verses he had conceived.

Before Shakspeare, as far as we can learn, began to write for the stage, Lope was a volunteer on-board the famous armada destined for the destruction of this country. And, not long before that period, as we are told by Cervantes himself,

in

in his Prologo to his Comedias, the Spanish stage was in a wretched condition. Comedies were pastoral dialogues, with interludes, in which the ribaldry of a black slave, the boasting of a coward, and the blunders of a Biscayner, resembling our Teague's bulls, formed the principal part. To them, it is said, we owe our Bobadil. All the apparatus of their theatre, says the same author, might be wrapped up in a bag;—being nothing more than four gilt leather skins, and as many false beards and heads of hair, with three or four sticks, or sheep-crooks. They had no changes of scenes; no passage for the actors in the center of the stage, the whole of which consisted of a few boards laid over benches. An old curtain, drawn across, divided the part where the actors dressed; and the musicians sang without the assistance of instruments.

While the Spanish theatre laboured under these disadvantages, a genius, who may be properly styled the Spanish Roscius, started up in the person of Lope de Rueda, whose dramatic pieces are still extant, and confer honour on his memory. This man was a gold-beater by trade; and surely it is praise sufficient for him to have Cervantes for his panegyrist, who declares that none ever equalled him as an actor, or in the natural turn of his dialogue and truth of character.

His prologues and interludes are distinguished by the name of Passos, compositions at this day known by the name of Loas Entremeses and Saenetes. Lope de Rueda died at Cordova, and, in consideration of his great merit, was interred in the cathedral between the two choirs.

Noharro, a successor of Rueda in acting, was an approved imitator of his master in the low comic.

mic. In his days the bag was withdrawn, and gave way to trunks, which held the stage-furniture.

Cervantes, soon after his redemption from slavery, in 1580, turned his studies to the theatre, and wrote *Los Tratos de Argel*, or The Humours of Algiers; and between twenty and thirty other comedies, which were acted, but never printed. —— The names of those plays, which were printed, are, *La grand Turquesca*, *La Batalla naval*, *La Jerusalem*, *La Amaranta o Mayo*, *El Bosque amoroso*, *La Arsinda*, and *La Confusa*. He was the first who divided the Spanish drama into three jornadas, or acts. He was likewise a strenuous defender of the antients, on which account he attacked his rival, Lope de Vega, with all his might; but the latter, by indulging the bent and humour of the people, and by being possessed of a rich and most exuberant fancy, with a just delineation of character, like the force of an impetuous torrent, bore down all before him. His invention was so fruitful, and his productions so rapid, that he did not give the public leisure to distinguish the efforts of genius from the wild sallies of intemperate fancy.

Calderone, who soon followed Lope de Vega, gave the finishing hand to the plan of his predecessor, and, with the same advantage of language and wit, debauched the taste of the people. In the scenes of this writer, the fair sex are taught to sacrifice every thing to the impulse of love, to despise the injunctions of parents, and yield to the arts of seduction. This author's wit is the more dangerous from being delivered in expressions the most captivating and beautiful. But this cannot be said of all Calderone's plays; some of of them I have read, which do not merit this severe censure.

Lope de Vega was so extraordinary a genius, that it is with difficulty we can quit a subject so agreeable. Some particulars of his life are singular and worth knowing.

When he was five years old, he could read Spanish and Latin, and make verses with fluency. At the age of twelve, he was master of the Latin tongue and a complete rhetorician; he could then, too, dance and fence with ease and dexterity, and sing in a tolerable taste. At his first entrance into life, he became an orphan with every pressure of distress. He was taken into the service of the Bishop of Aviler, in whose praise he wrote several pastorals, and made his first dramatic essay, in a comedy called *La Pastoral de Jacinto*.—Soon afterwards, we find him secretary to the famous Duke of Alva, whose praises he sang in his Arcadia. About this time he married a lady of fashion, on account of whose gallantries he fought a duel; and, having dangerously wounded his adversary, he fled to Valencia, where he resided several years. On his return to Madrid, he lost his wife; and, being seized with the military ardour, he went onboard the grand armada. In this expedition, so glorious to England and disgraceful to Spain, De Vega lost his brother, who was killed in a naval engagement.—Lope had his share in the general misfortune of his country, and appeared at Madrid without a single friend. The Count de Lemos, sensible of his merit, made him his secretary. He now ventured upon a second marriage with a woman of rank. This lady was Donna Juanna de Guardia, whom he soon after lost. Inconsolable with these afflictions, La Vega entered into the state ecclesiastical, and was ordained a priest. He still courted the muses, as the chief relaxation of his sorrows. He was now become so illustrious, that Pope Urban VIII. sent him a degree of doctor in divinity, and the cross of the order of Malta, added to a lucrative post in the apostolic chamber. This he enjoyed to his death, which happened in the seventy-third year of his age, to the great regret of the court and every learned man in the kingdom.—He was most magnificently interred at the expence of the Duke of Sesa, his patron and executor. The Duke invited to the interment all the grandees of the kingdom. The funeral obsequies lasted three days; all the clergy of the king's chapel assisted; three bishops officiated pontifically; three eminent orators exerted themselves in the praises of the deceased, with whom, when living, many princes gloried in being acquainted.

When Lope de Vega walked in the streets of Madrid, he was gazed at and followed as a prodigy. He was loaded with presents; by the rapid sale of his works, he accumulated a capital of 150,000 ducats, besides his annual income, of 1500 ducats, arising from his benefices and employments.

So great were the fertility of his genius, the readiness of his wit, rapidity of his thought, and animated expression, that there never was a poet in the world, either antient or modern, that could be compared to him. His lyric compositions and fugitive pieces, with his prose-essays, form a collection of fifty volumes; besides his dramatic works, in twenty-six volumes; exclusive of four hundred Autos sacramentales, all

which

which were successively brought on the stage. What is still more surprising, we have his own authority to say, that they formed the least part of what still remained in his closet. By exact computation, this author wrote twenty-one millions three hundred and sixteen thousand verses. So extraordinary was the quickness of his fancy, he would finish a play in twenty-four hours; and some comedies he completed in less than four hours. It was not, says my author, his fault, that some of his immediate successors had not his talents, and only imitated his imperfections; for the Spanish drama grew insupportable when deprived of the beauties of Lope. This was foreseen by Cervantes, who reproaches our poet with destroying the rules of the drama to court popular applause. And indeed Lope, in some verses which he published, owns the charge; the purport of which is, 'That he was sensible of the reproaches, which the critics of Italy and France would make him, for breaking through all rules to please an ignorant public; but, since they paid for it, they had a right to be pleased in their own way.'

But that, which gives the greatest lustre to the name of De Vega, is derived from his personal virtues, which were superior to his literary talents. His benevolence and charity towards the distressed were so great, that he ever extended his hand to the needy; insomuch that, notwithstanding his great wealth and large income, not more than six thousand ducats were found in his possession at his death.*

This

* For the account of the Spanish theatre, and the life of Lope de Vega, I am obliged to my friend, Mr. Bowle, of Idmiston;

Mr.

This much I thought was due to the memory of so great a genius, the contemporary of Shakspeare, and ranked with him in fame.

I have owned my inability to trace Beaumont and Fletcher in the plots, characters, and situations of the Spanish dramatists, though it can hardly be doubted, but that they would make use of that which they could so easily reach, and which they so well understood.

Of the fifty-four dramatic pieces, written by these great poets, two only at present preserve their rank on the stage, the Chances, and Rule a Wife and have a Wife. No writers, sure, ever experienced such a reverse of fortune! To be tumbled from the highest exaltation of fame to neglect and oblivion is a mortifying lesson to all successful writers!

Mr. Garrick was often called upon, by the admirers of our old bards, and more particularly by Mr. Colman, in a letter, addressed to him, containing reflections on our old English dramatic writers, not to confine his labour of love to Shakspeare, but to extend his plan, and to open the rich treasures of Fletcher, Jonson, and Massinger; and more especially to take into his theatrical roll those admirable plays, the Maid's Tragedy, King and no King, Philaster, the Elder Brother, and the City Madam. These, in the names of Burbage, Taylor, and Betterton, he conjured our great Roscius, to restore to the public. And here, I doubt, somebody might hint, it were to be wished that Mr. Colman had not employed the names of those celebrated old comedians

---

Mr. Hayley's copious notes to his Essay on epic Poetry; but more especially to some valuable letters of an English Traveller in Spain, published by R. Baldwin, Pater-noster Row.

dians as a powerful charm to prevail on Mr. Garrick to grant his requeſt, who never wiſhed to hear the name of any actor but one.

But this excellent friend of the playhouſe and players, Mr. Colman, not content with inforcing his arguments to convince the manager of the great powers of writing which lay dormant in theſe dramatiſts, twenty years ſince revived Philaſter, with great ſucceſs, at Drury-lane, in which he introduced to the public a young and great acting genius, and gave an opportunity to the accompliſhed Mrs. Yates to diſplay her talents in a new walk of elegant ſimplicity. Bonduca he reſtored, with approved alterations and much applauſe, at his theatre in the Haymarket.

Unwearied in his affection to this *par nobile fratrum*, ſome years ſince, Mr. Colman undertook the publication of an edition of their works in ten volumes octavo. In this he has carefully ſupplied the defects of former editions; nor has he omitted to do all poſſible juſtice to the commentators, Meſſrs. Theobald, Seward, and Symſon, whoſe merits he has candidly acknowledged, and has inſerted all ſuch notes of theirs as tend to illuſtrate the text of the authors. And, what is much to his reputation, he has not, in his criticiſms, indulged himſelf in the illiberal cuſtom of inſulting his predeceſſors.

The comedians, too, are obliged to this writer, for reſcuing *them* from the contempt and ſcorn thrown upon them by ſeveral editors of Shakſpeare. In one part of his preface, he candidly acknowledges that the ſtage owes its attraction to the actor as well as the author, with this happy illuſtration: ' For, if the able performer will not contribute to give a poliſh and brilliancy o the work, it will be, like the rough diamond, obscured and disregarded.' In another part of it, he endeavours to heal the wounds made by the stings of the irritable Pope: ' Cibber, idle Cibber,' says this agreeable author, ' wrote for the stage with more success than Pope. Æschylus, Sophocles, Plautus, and Terence, were soldiers and freemen; Shakspeare and Moliere were actors.'

Mr. Colman perhaps had forgotten, that Æschylus was a great actor as well as a renowned soldier; that he not only acted the principal parts in his tragedies, but composed the music for them, ordered what particular dresses should be worn, and projected all the machinery; and, lastly, that he distributed the parts to the rest of the players, so marked and noted that they could not possibly mistake the proper pronunciation of every line. Sophocles understood the art of acting; but the weakness of his voice prevented him from joining the profession of player to that of author.

But, to return to Beaumont and Fletcher. After all which the warmest admirers of these writers can say in their commendation, the great preference, given by the public to Shakspeare, may be established on a lasting foundation, without in the least diminishing their real and intrinsic merit.

I have ever looked on Beaumont and Fletcher as the disciples, or rather the dramatic offspring, of Shakspeare; and such an offspring as will ever reflect great honour on the parent.

His first uncontested dramatic piece* is fixed, by Mr. Malone, to the year 1591, when Shakspeare

* Love's Labour lost.

speare had arrived to the age of twenty-five. Fletcher was then in his 14th or 15th year, and Beaumont a child of six years old. The earlieſt of their productions cannot, I believe, be traced farther back than early in the reign of James I.
——— Notwithſtanding what is ſaid by Seward of their predilection for Ben Jonſon, and Beaumont's imitation of his manner, in perſonifying paſſions rather than in drawing characters, I am perſuaded that they both chiefly formed themſelves on Shakſpeare, many of whoſe admired plays had been acted long before the fame of Jonſon was generally known. They, as well as the great poet, took their plots from hiſtory and romance. Their characters, like his, are as various as nature could produce, and, in moſt of their pieces, admirably and faithfully delineated; their ſentiments are tender, pathetic, and forcible, as plot, ſituation, and character, require. Their dialogue is univerſally allowed to be free, elegant, pleaſant, and witty; in general more adapted to the converſation of gentlemen than Shakſpeare's. And this excellence we may obviouſly conjecture to have proceeded from their higher rank in life and more poliſhed education; the ſons of a biſhop and judge could command a choicer ſet of companions than a poor player. But, though I grant their ſcenes abound more in liberal and high-ſeaſoned dialect than Shakſpeare's, yet, whenever he thinks proper to introduce wits, and treat his audience with gay converſe, he is not only equal, but ſuperior, to his imitators. For whom will they match with the ſprightly Mercutio, or the humorous Benedic? To ſay nothing of the pleaſantries of the amiable Roſalind, what dialogue can be put in competi-

competition with the lively, witty, varied mirth, the rapidly-facetious and laugh-winning repartees, of the Prince of Wales and Jack Falstaff?

It must also be allowed, that the scenes of these twin poets are often blotted with unpardonable licentiousness and stained with vile obscenity. It is not enough to say, in their defence, that the poets of their age wrote in the same style. They have gone beyond all that I ever read of those times in illiberal freedom. Seward, indeed, coldly owns, that Shakspeare does not offend, in this point, so often as they do. But I will be bold to assert, that compared with these authors, he is modest and chaste, and writes like an anchoret. A dispassionate and candid reader cannot help suggesting, that the scenes of our great dramatist seem to have been acted before different auditors than those of Beaumont and Fletcher. Innumerable instances of unlimited licentiousness may be produced from many of their plays. I need only refer the reader to the Captain,—the Scornful Lady, since altered, much for the better, to the Capricious Lady, at the desire, as I have heard, of an eminent actress, who performed the principal character,—and the Custom of the Country. To this freedom of style they in some measure owed the success of their dramas in the reign of Charles II. They approached nearer, in dialogue and character, to the colour of the times, than the plays of any other author.

But there is a wide difference, in the management of their plots, between Shakspeare and Beaumont and Fletcher. Those of the former are altogether as improbable as the latter. But under

under his direction, improbability lessens imperceptibly; the superstructure is so beautiful, that you forget the foundation. You survey the whole building with such delight, that you have not leisure to think of the enchanted ground on which it stands.

Let me instance only the Merchant of Venice. Can any story be devised more strange and absurd than a bond with a forfeiture of a pound of flesh? But, when once you have admitted that into your belief, how does the poet, by the skilful texture of the scene, alarm your mind and work on your passions! Notwithstanding the very odious character of the Jew, Shakspeare has the art to interest you, for a time, in his favour. In the third act, we have a scene, restored to the stage by the superior taste of Charles Macklin, to whom indeed we owe the play as it now stands, in which the Jew's private calamities make some tender impressions on the audience; but the author, aware of the consequence of indulging this pity, rouses them to a just knowledge of his character, by making Shylock, in the midst of his private distresses, give vent to his inveterate hatred to the Merchant, whose blood he determines to spill. The story of the caskets is as romantic as any tale of knight-errantry: in the hands of our enchanter it passes for true history. In the fourth act of the play, a young lady, in the dress of a lawyer, imposes upon the high court of justice, and saves the life of the Merchant, by the help of a quibble: but the whole is conducted in such a powerful manner as to justify the most discerning spectators in the approbation of the writer.

Let

Let us now take a view of Fletcher's Wife for a Month, in which there are some justly-admired scenes, well-drawn characters, and much excellent satire.

There are, in this play, as well as in the Merchant of Venice, two plots: the putting up a lady by auction, as a wife for a month, and the recovering a sick king by a dose of poison.

Frederic, the King's brother, during the illness of the latter, takes upon him the government of the state. His passions are vicious in the extreme: he plots the death of the King, and attempts the chastity of a noble and virtuous lady, the sister of his minister, who, so far from endeavouring to curb his master's appetite, offers himself the willing pander in the management of the infamous business. Evanthe, the lady, is betrothed to Valerio, a young nobleman of great and amiable qualities.—Frederic consents that the lover shall marry the lady, but under the injunction that he shall not cohabit with her more than a month. To complete the misery of the unhappy pair, Sorano, the minister, suggests to his master the cruel plan of obliging Valerio not to enjoy his wife, under the forfeiture of her life. The struggles, arising in the breast of Valerio from this injunction, are well described; an after-scene, between the husband and wife, terminates much to the honour of the lady. The King insults Valerio on his situation, and receives from him such keen reproaches, as no tyrant, invested with unlimited power, would tolerate. Evanthe dismisses an attendant, who had always talked to her mistress in the language of the brothel, and had given her such advice as becomes the mouth only of a most abandoned prostitute.

tute. A warm scene ensues between Evanthe and the King, where nobleness of spirit is blended with vulgarity of language. Another interview follows, between the husband and wife, where Evanthe is equally violent and submissive. She is now put up to auction, the wife for a month. Three low wretches bid for her, but retreat as soon as they know the condition of marriage. Valerio, in disguise, with a forged story of his death, puts in his claim. As he is going off with her, he is called back by the tyrant, who, on the appearance of Alphonso, his elder brother, cured by the poison given by Sorano, is deposed, and the lovers are made happy. Of Alphonso's delirium, and the impropriety of amplifying in such a situation, I have spoken at large towards the latter end of my remarks on King John.—————
I need not say any thing of the conduct of this play, but the manners are still worse. That a young lady, in the pride of youth and bloom of beauty, such as Evanthe, should have warm desires, when ascending the nuptial bed, is what we expect; but surely modest reluctance in the lady will heighten her charms, and prove the best incentive to the lover. It is, in the language of Shakspeare,

> ——————— A pudency so rosy,
> As would warm old Saturn.

But Evanthe is so eager, that she stimulates her husband:

EVANTHE.

EVANTHE.

——— ——— To bed, then:
——— ——— Fie, my lord!
Will you put a maid to't to teach you what to do?
Are you so cold a lover?

Much more, and still warmer, is urged by Evanthe; which is certainly extremely natural. But why not draw the curtains of the marriage-bed? Why will these writers, like Mrs. Behn, ' Fairly put all characters to bed, *and shew them there?*' However, this I should have passed over, in our authors, as pardonable, from a young, exuberant, and vigorous, fancy, and suited to a tempting situation. But how the play of the Captain could be tolerated by any spectators, it is impossible not to ask.

Lelia, a lewd woman, tempts her own father, knowing him to be such, to her bed. Struck with horror, he shudders at the thoughts of so shocking a crime. She persists; and, by argument, strives to reconcile him to the commission of incest.—This infamous woman, instead of being punished, is married to a gentleman. It is inconceivable how any audience could support scenes so unlike any of Shakspeare, Ben Jonson, and Massinger.

After all I have said of the conduct and manners, in several plays, of these writers, I wish not to depreciate their real merits, or to blend their faults with their excellencies. When their superfluous and rotten branches are lopped away, there will be sufficient remaining to flourish to all ages. I am firmly of opinion, that Beaumont and Fletcher are not so much excelled by their master's power of genius as his perfect skill in

conducting

conducting his scenes to produce a happy effect. No man knew so thoroughly the measure of theatrical ground as himself. This seems to have been his great study.

Methinks I see him sitting, unnoticed, amongst the spectators, with deep attention observing the progress of the plot, the consequence of character, the influence of passion, the result of situation, and the general effect of the whole. No writer ever knew how to interest the minds of an audience, which is the great art of dramatic writing, like Shakspeare.

Before I close what I have to say concerning those eminent writers, Beaumont and Fletcher, I cannot help observing, that the outcry, raised against those spectators who did not relish the beauties of the Faithful Shepherdess, is not so well founded as is generally imagined. Ben Jonson's censure is indeed almost ridiculous. How could he expect a mixed and rude audience, such as that of London was in his time, composed of a few good judges and a rabble of ignorants, as he himself describes them in his prologues and inductions, could taste the beauties of so delicate and exquisite a composition, which, for learned allegory, pastoral manners and variety and harmony of poetry, may challenge all that Greece or Italy, antient and modern, have produced? But it ought to be remembered, that, where characters are shewn on the stage, of which the spectators have no resemblances in their minds, it is impossible they can be interested for their fate.

Without considerable alterations, fine music, gay scenes, beautiful decorations, and excellent performers, I would not hazard the Faithful Shepherdess upon a London stage in these cultivated times. The universities of Oxford and Cambridge would, I believe, reflect honour on their own judgment by applauding so elegant a performance. It will give strength to my argument, in favour of the superior skill of Shakspeare to govern the spirit of the public, to observe, that the pastoral part of the Winter's Tale, Florizel and Perdita, without any assistance from the antients, or of modern Italy, perpetually triumphs over the passions of an English auditory.

I entirely agree, with the last editors of Beaumont and Fletcher, that Shakspeare was not an associate with Fletcher in writing the Two noble Kinsmen. The assertion, that it was so, is unsupported by any other evidence than the credit of a title-page. The publisher knew very well, that, besides the intrinsic merit of the piece, the names of Shakspeare and Fletcher would operate as a superior charm to vend the Two noble Kinsmen.

Beaumont and Fletcher seemed rather to have envied the superior success and merit of Shakspeare than to have entertained any wish to cultivate his friendship. His name is mentioned in no poem of Beaumont; nor did Fletcher, though he survived our great bard nine years, and the publication of his works, by Hemings and Condell, two years, join the chorus of the poets who sacrificed to his manes.

This

This I do not give the reader as a certain proof that they were not acquainted, and did not live on friendly terms; but I see no reason to rob Beaumont and Fletcher of the honour of writing the Two noble Kinsmen, a piece which deserves the best encomium the best writer can bestow. But the story of Palamon and Arcite is better adapted to that kind of poetry which the Italians call Romanza, and which celebrates acts of chivalry,—such as Amadigi, Orlando innamorato, Orlando furioso, and such indeed as it was in the original of Chaucer,——than to a dramatic fable.

It has not been observed, I believe, that three queens supplicating, in this play, are borrowed from the chorus of Argive ladies in the Ικετιδες of Euripides.

Downs has placed Rule a Wife and have a Wife second in succession to the Humourous Lieutenant; with which play the king's company opened Drury-lane theatre, the 8th of April, 1663. It was performed twelve times successively.

Hart and Mohun were much celebrated for their excellent action in this comedy: the latter in Leon, and the former in Michael Perez. Mrs. Marshal, the greatest tragic actress of that company, represented Margaretta; and Mrs. Boutell, celebrated for the gentler parts in tragedy, such as Aspasia in the Maid's Tragedy, Statira in Alexander, played Estifania with applause.

As I have not before me the novel of Cervantes, whence the plot of this comedy is taken, it is not in my power to say what particular use our authors made of their original. Whether we examine the main plot of the comedy, or the epi-
sodical

sodical part of it, we shall pronounce it a very entertaining and truly dramatic piece. The honest scheme of Leon, a man of honour and courage, to rescue a fine woman, of large fortune, from her own perverse will, from pursuing the gratification of inordinate appetite and passion, under the veil of a husband whom she purposed to make the blind for her pleasures, is well conceived and artfully conducted. Michael Perez, the military coxcomb, who fancies himself such an object of attraction, that every fine lady who views him must immediately fall in love, is, by an artful intriguing girl, brought by ludicrous contrivances, to a just sense of his folly. Cacafogo was intended, as I have been told by the old actors, a rival to Falstaff. If so, there never was so complete a triumph over impotent rivalship as that of Shakspeare. Cacafogo resembles the fat knight in nothing but cowardice. Though Falstaff ran away as fast as his legs could carry him, *when there was an hundred upon poor four*,* yet he was never so disgraced as to take a kicking.

When Rule a Wife and have a Wife was represented, above half a century since, at Drury-lane, the elder Mills acted Leon, Wilks Perez, Mrs. Horton Margaretta, Estifania by Mrs. Oldfield. Booth certainly would have been an admirable Leon; for he had enough of comic humour for the assumed folly of the part, and abundance of manly fire and noble action to display, when he broke through the cloud of his disguise, and proved himself the vindicator of his own honour, and the worthy husband of the lady he had married. But Booth avoided a contention with the impetuous Wilks, the avowed patron of Mills; he

* Henry IV. First Part, act II.

he was, besides, too indolent to struggle for those parts which apparently claimed his animated exertion.

The comic humour of Wilks was so intimately blended with the elegant manners of the gentleman, that his performance of this part commonly called the Copper Captain, was esteemed one of his best-represented characters. Mrs. Oldfield's Estifania was an excellent counterpart of comic spirit to the sprightly humour of Wilks. When Ryan and Mrs. Younger, about the same time, acted these parts at the theatre of Lincoln's-inn Fields, it was universally allowed, that, though they were comedians of great merit, they fell infinitely short of their competitors.——When Oldfield drew the pistol from her pocket, pretending to shoot Perez, Wilks drew back as if grealy terrified, and, in a tremulous voice, uttered, *What! thy own husband!* Oldfield replied, with an archness of countenance and half-shut eye, *Let mine own husband, then, be in his own wits,* in a tone of voice so exactly in imitation of his, that the theatre was in a tumult of applause. Woodward and Mrs. Pritchard, Mr. King and Mrs. Abington, without having seen these great performers, have very happily diverted the audience in this and the other scenes of the play.

In the year 1759, Mr. Garrick revived this comedy. It was wished, by Mr. Mossop and his friends, that the two principal parts might have been divided between him and the manager; Mossop Leon, and Perez Garrick; but Roscius determined otherwise. Tho' he was an improper figure for the man whom a lady chooses by her eye, he determined to act Leon, and give the other part to Woodward. Garrick, indeed, might plead, that

that Major Mohun was admired in Leon, though certainly not a perſon of large figure, as we underſtand by what Nat. Lee ſaid to him on his acting Mithridates: 'Thou little man of mettle! if I ſhould write a hundred plays, I would write a part for thy mouth.'

Mrs. Cibber inſiſted upon injuring her own conſequence, if that were poſſible, by acting Eſtifania. But Melpomene could not transfer herſelf into Thalia; after a few nights trial of her comic abilities, ſhe reſigned Eſtifania. It was then delivered to Mrs. Pritchard, who acted it with much applauſe.

Mrs. Clive had an undoubted claim to this part, as the ſuperior actreſs of the theatre. But neither maſter nor man, neither Garrick nor Woodward, wiſhed to ſee her in this play; and I firmly believe they kept her out of it from a tribute which they paid to her ſuperior abilities.

Though Garrick's perſon did not preſent us with the true figure of Leon, and he was obliged to curtail ſeveral lines which deſcribed him as the author intended him to be in repreſentation, yet his performance was ſo much in truth and nature, that the ſpectators wanted neither height nor bulk. He wore the diſguiſe of folly, to intrap the cautious Margaretta, ſo exactly and humorouſly, that he preſented the complete picture of a Wittol. When he put on the man of courage, and aſſerted the honeſt rights of a huſband, no one of a more brawny or ſinewy figure could have manifeſted more fire or beautiful animation. The warmth of his ſpirit was ſo judiciouſly tempered, his action ſo correſpondent to his utterance, his whole deportment ſo ſignificant and important, that

that I think I never saw him more universally captivate the eyes and ears of an applauding theatre.

The players seem, in general, to confine the word *feeling* to the tender and pathetic parts of tragedy. I shall beg leave to extend it to rage and horror, as well as grief and love, in tragedy; to the representation of mirth, gaiety, pleasanty, and humour, in comedy. I understand the rightly *feeling* a part to be the comedian's properly becoming, in voice, action, look, deportment, any attitude or situation of character whatever. When the Duke of Medina, in this play, said to Leon, at the close of that important scene in the third act,

> I pray, sir, use your wife well,—

those, who remember Garrick in this situation, will recollect with pleasure his most expressive look and action, when, sheathing his sword, he uttered this pertinent reply,

> My own humanity will teach me this.

END OF VOL. II.

INDEX to VOL. II.

A.

ABINGTON, (Mrs.) and Mr. King, 263.
Acheron and Acheneen, 107.
Actress, the first that appeared on a London stage, 237.
Æschylus, 88, 92, 100, 106, 119, 252.
———, Sophocles, Plautus, Terence, Shakspeare, and Moliere, 252.
Æsopus, Moliere, and Colley Cibber, 142, 143.
——— and Roscius, 140.
——— his public spirit, 141.
——— his riches and death, 143.
Alchemist, 66.
——————— bad catastrophe, 67.
——————— Abel Drugger, as acted by The. Cibber, Mr. Garrick, and Weston, 66, 67.
All's Well that ends Well, 4, 32.
——————————————— the fable unpromising, *ibid*.
——————————————— revived in 1741, *ibid*.
——————————————— by Garrick in 1757, and the distribution of the parts, 6.
——————————————— passages explained, 9, 10, 15, 16, 19—25, 31, 32.
——————————————— scene of Parolles, 25, &c.
Anecdote of a country gentleman, 82.
Antony and Cleopatra, 217, 247.
——————————— Ben Jonson's ridicule of it, 218.
——————————— Dr. Johnson's opinion of it, *ibid*.
——————————— revived by Garrick in 1760, 240.
——————————— passages explained, 219, 221—241.

Antony's servant and Brutus, 155.
——— oration, 156.
——— well paid for his oratory, 157.
Arbuthnot, 144, 152, 153, 157.
Aristocracy and oligarchy, 148.
——————— the worst of all governments, 151:
Assassination of Julius Cæsar, the difficulty of representing it, 153.
Athenian stage, 235.
Augustus, 220.

B.

Baddeley, commended, 45.
Baretti, 238.
Barrett, 12.
Barrenness, a curse, 15.
Barry, 83.
——— his powers, 157.
——— his Lear, 181, 213
Beaumont and Fletcher, 237, 259.
———————————— their plots taken from Spanish novels, and probably from Spanish plays, 243
———————————— only two of their plays preserved on the stage, 250.
———————————— their composition described, 253.
———————————— their licentious style, 254.
———————————— Shakspeare compared to them modest, *ibid.*
———————————— envious of Shakspeare, 260.
Berry, 5, 6, 42, 81.
Bessus, a pander as well as a coward, 28.
Betterton, 72, 168, 177, 178.
——— his Macbeth, 81
Bobadil, an original character, 34.
Boheme's person, voice, and manner, 178, 179.
Boileau and Lully, 8.

Boman,

INDEX.

Boman, 62.
Bonduca, 250.
Booth, 65, 81, 82, 117, 178, 180, 262.
───── and Quin in Brutus, 160.
───── in uttering Lear's curse, inferior to Garrick, 180.
───── and Boheme in Lear, 178, 179.
───── and Garrick in Lear, 212, 213.
───── and Mrs Oldfield, 240.
───── his Antony in All for Love, *ibid.*
Bounty and generosity of Marc Antony, 232, &c.
Boutell, (Mrs.) 261.
Boys acting women's parts, 237.
Bracken, 223.
Brantome quoted, 203, 204.
Brown, 196.
Brunswick, house of, renounced all pretensions to royal witchcraft, 116.
Brutus and Cassius, 160, 161.
───── his character, 164, 165.
Buchanan, 78, 101, 108, 125.
───── and Hollingshead, 76.
Buckingham and Foote, 76.
───── his two tragedies taken from Shakspear's Julius Cæsar, 131.
Burbage, 51, 209.
───── supposed to have been the original Macbeth, 81.
Butler, (Mrs) 6, 61, 62.

C.

Cæsar's urbanity, 146.
───── question concerning his death, 146, 147.
───── abilities and clemency, 147, 150, 151.
───── perfidy of the conspirators against him, 150, 151.
Calderone, 246.

Captain, Scornful Lady, and Custom of the country, 254.
Carlo Buffone, 47.
Cartwright and Mohun, 65.
Casca in Julius Cæsar, 136, 137.
Cashel, 83.
——— anecdote of him and an insidious rival, 83, 84.
——— his death and that of his rival, 85.
Cassius's character, 137.
Catiline by Ben Jonson, 15.
——— condemned originally, 55.
——— revived by Charles Hart, supposed at the instigation of Buckingham, Dorset, &c. 55.
——— tedious, 56.
——— Cicero's speeches immoderately long, 56, 57.
——— character of Cicero rejected by Mohun for Cethegus, 56, 57.
Celia and dame Kitely, 57.
Cervantes, 244.
——— his account of the Spanish theatre, 245.
——— his plays, 245, 256.
——— an opposer of Lope de la Vega, 246.
Chapman and Berry commended, 5.
Charles I. and Mr. Hyde, 230.
Chesterfield and Quin, 228.
Churchill and Ben Jonson, 51.
Cibber, 6, 117, 143, 154, 241.
Cibber, (Theophilus,) 5, 66.
——— (Mrs.) her Cordelia, 208.
——————— in comedy misplaced, 264.
Cicero, 135, 137, 140, 141, 150, 220.
——— and Roscius, 143, 144.
Clarke, 188.
Clement, Downright, and Brainworm, 34.
Cleopatra's noble preparation for death, 238.
——————— whether killed by poison or the aspic, *ibid.*

Cleopatra's

INDEX.

Cleopatra's character, *ibid.*
Cleveland, (dutchess of,) 154.
Clive, (Mrs.) 62, 264.
Clown, or fool, 10—13.
———————— his occupation, 11, 12.
———————— described in Twelfth Night, 12.
Collins, 48,
Colman, 64, 168, 172, 250, 251, 252.
———— his edition of Beaumont and Fletcher, 251.
———— obligations of the comedians to him, *ibid.*
Connoisseur, 90.
Cordelia and Edgar in Lear, 169, 170, &c.
Corvino, in Volpone, as acted by Cibber and Mills, 61, 62.
Countryman in Antony and Cleopatra, 238.
Cowardice in the abstract, no proper subject for mirth, 29.
Cynthia's revels, by Ben Jonson, 49, 50.

D.

Dagger-scene in Macbeth, 88.
Davenant, 71, 89, 90, 94.
Davies, 6.
——— (Mrs.) 6, 208, 209.
Delane, 6,
——— his death, 45.
Delicacy of the Roman ear, 142.
Demosthenes, 156.
Dennis's thunder, 36.
Deprivation of sight, a Norman punishment, 196.
Diggs, (Leonard,) 38, 129, 167.
——————————— his verses on Jonson's Volpone, Silent Woman and Alchemist, 58.
Distraction and recovery of Lear, 212—214.
Dodd, 45.
Dodsley, 236.

Doll Common in the Alchemist, as acted by Mrs. Clive and Mrs. Pritchard, 68.
Don Sebastian, by Dryden, 28.
Donald, governor of Foris, and his wife, 100.
Dorset (Earl of,) his epilogue to Every man in his Humour, 38.
Dover-cliff, 202.
Downs, 167, 168.
Downs in an error, 40, 46.
——— an anecdote from him, 94, 95.
Dryden, 63, 97, 130, 151, 162, 163, 164, 169.
——— his All for Love, 218, 219, 233, 240, 241.
Duffus, (King,) 74, 100.

E.

Edwards, 222.
Edgar's disguise in Lear, 189.
Elizabeth and the Earl of Essex, 31.
English epicures, 121.
English and Scotch, ancient enmity between them; compared with that of the Ombi and Tentyritæ, two nations of Egypt, 122.
Eros and Ventidius compared, 233.
Euripides, 163, 164.
Every Man in his Humour, 33—52.
——————————— its particular merit, 33.
——————————— the prologue, 36, 37.
——————————— revived after the Restoration, 37.
——————————— Lord Dorset's epilogue on its revival, 38.
——————————— revived by Garrick, 41.
——————————— merits of the several actors, ibid.
Every Man out of his Humour, 46, 50.
——————————— account of some of the characters, 47.

F.

F.

Faithful Shepherdefs, 259.
Falstaff, 231.
——— and Beffus, 29.
——— and Sir Epicure Mammon, 67.
Farmer, (Dr) 21, 94.
Fenton, 79, 225.
Fleetwood, 5.
Fletcher, 13.
Fontaines, (Abbé de,) 132.
Fool in Lear, 172.
Franklin, 182.
French hofe, 94.
French, Spanish, and Italian theatre, 238.
Froiffart, 87.
Fulvia, 219, 220.
——— her death, 220.

G.

Garrick, 6, 26, 29, 66, 67, 72, 74, 83, 98, 137, &c.
——— his care and pains in the revival of Every Man in his Humour, 41—43.
——— his intention to revive Volpone, 62.
——— and Mrs. Pritchard in the Tragedy of Macbeth, 93, 105.
——— his opinion of the part of Macbeth, 105.
——— and Abbé le Blanc, 162.
——— his Lear, 180, 190, 207, 209, 213.
——— and Mrs. Yates, 240.
——— urged to revive the plays of Beaumont and Fletcher, and Maffinger, 250.
——— his great fkill in Leon, 263, 264.
Gillow, 153.
Glofter, in K. Lear, the manner of putting out his eyes, 197.
——— as acted by Quin, Hulet, Mills, Berry, and Davies, 198.
Goodman, 154.
——— a highwayman, *ibid*.

Gracchi,

Gracchi, 148.
Greek tragedians, 207.
Griffin, 153.
——— and Jonson, the actor, 67.
Gurdon, 125.

H.

Hall, 16.
Hammer, 229.
Harper and Love, 68.
Harrington, Sir John, his witty answer to James I. 75.
Hart, his excellence in Catiline, 56.
——— and Mohun, their excellence in Brutus and Cassius, in Shakspeare's Julius Cæsar, 130.
Havard, 210.
Helen's description of Parolles, in All's Well that ends Well, 7.
——— delicacy, 17.
——— ring, 31.
Henderson, 45.
Hill's Roman Revenge, 133, 134.
——————————— quoted, 131, 132.
Horton, (Mrs.) 61, 262.
Humour defined, 48.
Hurd, (Dr.) and Carlo Buffone, 47, 48.
Hymns of Orpheus, 92.

J.

James I. 69, 70.
——— and Sir John Harrington, 75.
Jevon, 153.
Incantation of witches, 110, 111.
Incest, an improper subject for a play, 27, 28.
Johnson, (Dr.) 19, 31, 68, 71, 101, 123, 136, 160, 170, &c.

Johnson

INDEX.

Johnson (Dr.) in a mistake, 19.
———— and Steevens, 9, 20, 21.
Jonson, the actor, 61, 65, 135.
———— his death, 65.
Jonson, (Ben) 53, 66, 218.
———— and Fletcher, 13.
———— not averse from mirth in tragedy, 14.
———— his Sejanus and Catiline, 14, 15.
———— his language, 33, 34.
———— assisted in his Sejanus by Shakspeare, 53.
———— his translations from the classics, 52, 54, 65,
———— his ignorance of decency and decorum, 54, 55.
———— his defence of Silius commended, 55.
———— his ladies, 57.
———— acquainted with the D. of Buckingham when a boy, 59.
———— his Volpone, 61.
———— his Silent Woman, 63.
———— difficulty in acting his characters, 59, 64.
———— his plays obsolete, 64.
———— his Alchemist, 66.
———— his panegyric of Q. Elizabeth, 48, 49.
———— his Poetaster, a satire on the players, 50, 51.
———— his As you find it, 50.
———— his envy and malice towards Shakspeare, 35, &c.
———— his panegyric on Shakspeare, 37.
———— his knowledge of Roman manners, 57.
———— how esteemed by his contemporaries, 57, 58.
———— some of his plays acted by children, 65, &c.
———— his contention with Shakspeare, 111.

INDEX.

Jonſon, (Ben) quotation from his Queens Maſque, 111.
——————— attire of his witches, 114.
Iſocrates and Demoſthenes, 156.
Julius Cæſar, 99, 125, 165, 234.
——————— its reception when originally acted, 129.
——————— why not acted under Garrick's management, 137.
——————— paſſages explained, 136, 138, 139, 147, 155—161.
——————— the concluſion, 165.
——————— the actors in it, 153.
——————— ſhort character of it, 165.
Juvenal, 122.

K.

Kempe, 51.
Kenrick, 77.
Kent in Lear, 187.
King and no King, intended to have been revived by Garrick, 27; why thrown aſide, 27, 28.
King's evil, 115 & ſeq.
Kitely and Mr. Ford, 34.
Kynaſton, 153.

L.

Lady Macbeth and Clytemneſtra, 80.
Lambard, 75.
Lear, 167—216.
—— ſuppoſed not to be originally much admired, 167, 178, 197.
—— fewer editions of it than many of Shakſpeare's plays, 167.
—— not often acted in its priſtine ſtate, 168.
—— Addiſon's and Richardſon's opinion of the cataſtrophe, 170.

Lear,

INDEX.

Lear, passages explained, 171, 172, 175,—177, 182—186, 189, 192, 194, 198---202, 204, &c. *seq.*
────── a scene judiciously restored by Mr. Colman, 173.
────── character of the Bastard, *ibid.*
────────────── gentleman-usher. 176, 202.
────── happy restoration of a passage, 90.
────── Tate's additional scenes, 212.
────── a short comparison of it with other plays, 214.
Lee, 129.
Leigh, 153.
Lelia and her father in the Captain, 258.
Lesly, 125.
Lewis XI. and St. Francis of Paul, 116.
Ligarius in Julius Cæsar, acted by Bowman, 138.
Literature in the reigns of Elizabeth and James I. 57.
Lloyd's verses on the ghost of Banquo in Macbeth, 104.
Locke, 97.
────── a master of music, 71, 72.
Lope de Rueda, the Spanish Roscius, 245.
────────────── his death, *ibid.*
Lope de la Vega, 244.
────────────── his uncommon genius, 247.
────────────── remarkable passages in his life, 247—249.
────────────── his marriage and duel, 247.
────────────── a soldier on board the Armada, 244, 247.
────────────── second marriage, 247.
────────────── his misfortunes, 248.
────────────── ordained priest, *ibid.*
────────────── honoured with a degree by pope Urban, *ibid.*
────────────── his death and funeral, *ibid.*
────────────── gazed at when walking in the streets, *ibid.*
────────────── his great riches, 249.
────────────── his quickness in composition, *ibid.*

Lope

INDEX.

Lope de la Vega, his reasons for breaking through the rules of the drama, 249.
———————— his extensive benevolence and charity, *ibid.*
Lord-mayor of London and Lord Burleigh, 236.
Love in Sir Epicure Mammon, 68.
Lowin, 51, 63.
Lucian's dialogues, 60.
Lully, Swift, and Lord Rivers, 8, 9.
Luxury of the Romans, 151, 152.

M.

Macbeth, 69—126.
————— the author's supposed design in writing this tragedy, 70.
————— altered by Davenant, 71.
————— restored by Garrick, 73.
————— an admirable sermon against murder, 93.
————— when first represented, 110.
————— passages explained, 74, 75, 76, 77, 78, 79, 80, 87, 89, 91, 94, 95, 98, 101, 104, 106, 108, 114, 115, 117, 118, 119, 120, 122, 125.
Macduff, as acted by Wilks, 117, and Ryan, 118.
————— hints to the actor of that part, 96, 124.
————— his character, 117.
Macklin, 96, 143, 255.
————— and The. Cibber, 5.
————— his opinion of Boheme's Lear, 179.
————— (Miss) 6.
Malone, 110, 107, 252.
Mammon in the Alchemist, 67.
Marshall, (Mrs.) 261.
Massinger's Unnatural Combat, 28.
————— Bashful Lover, 191.
Master Stephen and Master Slender, 34.
Masque of Queens, by Ben Jonson, 111.
————————— quoted, 111, 112, 113.
May's Cleopatra, 218.

Measure

INDEX.

Measure for Measure, 231.
Mechanics alike in Rome and England, 134, 135.
Medburne and the popish plot, 40.
———— his death, *ibid*.
Merchant of Venice, 255.
Mercutio, Benedic, and Rosalind, 253.
Middleton, 16.
Mills, (the elder) 61, 69, 241.
———————— unequal to the part of Macbeth, 81.
————————, Wilks, Booth, Mrs. Oldfield, Ryan, and Mrs. Younger, 263.
Mills, the younger, 61, 69.
———————— his Julius Cæsar, 154.
Milward, 4, 6, 62.
———— his character of Lusignan, 5:
———— his death, 4.
———— and Delane, 6.
———— his excellence in Antony, 157, 158.
Minors, (Miss,) since Mrs. Walker, 42.
Minshew, 202.
Mohun, his excellence in Cethegus in Catiline, 56, 57.
——— commended by Downs and Rochester, 130.
——— and Lee, 264.
Moliere, 142, 143.
———— and Lully; Garrick and Foote, 8.
Montague, (Mrs.) 126, 165.
Morose, in the Silent Woman, 63.
Mosca, in Volpone, as acted by Wilks and W. Mills, 62.
Mossop, 82, 83.
———— desires to act Leon in Rule a Wife and have a Wife, 263.
———— opposed by Garrick, *ibid*.
Mountfort, 153.
Mullus, a fish much valued by the Romans, 152.
Mysteries and Moralities, 11.

N. Nero,

N.

Nero, an actor, 139.
────── ──── his fear of an audience, 139, 140.
Nicholls, Mr. 116, 117.
Noharro, 245, 246.
Nokes, 95.

O.

Oldfield, (Mrs.) 263.
Osborne, 122.
Othello, 221.

P.

Palamon and Arcite, 261.
Palmer, 41.
────── his marriage and death, 42, 43.
────── commended, 45.
────── the late Palmer and the present, 67.
Parolles in All's Well that ends Well, compared with Bessus in King and no King, 25.
────── admirable to the last, 30.
Paulus Jovius, 244.
Pavy, one of the children of the revels, 65.
Pennant, 123.
Phædra and Hippolytus, 28.
Philaster, 250, 251.
Philip of Macedon compared to a sponge, 80.
Physicians in England, France, and Germany, 16.
Pity, beautifully described, 79.
Players must obey audiences, 141.
Pliny, 153.
Plutarch, 128, 129.
Poetaster, 50.

Poetaster, conjectures concerning the actors ridiculed in it, 51.
Poisoning-girdle, 75.
Polymnestor and Oedipus, 196, 197.
Pope, 21, 36, 202, 218.
Porter, (Mrs.) 96, 241.
Powell, (Geo.) 82, 209.
——— (Wm.) 180.
——————— his Lear, 181.
Power of certain worthless characters, 7.
Prince of Wales and Falstaff, 254.
Pritchard, (Mrs.) 6, 68, 186, 264.
Pro-consuls, or governors of Roman provinces, 149.

Q.

Quin, 45, 61, 82, 136, 137, 161, 162.
——— jealous of the applause given to Bowman, 138.
——— his Lear, 179.

R.

Rabelais, 204.
——— ——— Lucian, and Tom Brown, 196.
Reason for Macbeth's treason, 78.
Reddish, 210.
Rehearsal, 59, 65.
Rich, 44.
Riccoboni, 12.
Ridout, (Mrs.) 5.
Rivers, (Lord,) 8.
Roberts, 8.
Rochester, 56.
——— his character of Mohun, 130.
Romans, their situation at Cæsar's death, 151, 152, 153.
Roman actors, their indefatigable application, 139.
——————————— their dress, 140.

INDEX.

Roman actors, limited to particular parts, 142.
——— slaves, 151, 152.
Roscius, a rival of Cicero in gesticulation, 143.
——— the great teacher of acting, 144.
——— his character by Cicero, *ibid.*
——— his death, *ibid.*
——— Q. Catulus's opinion concerning him, 144, 145.
Ross and Palmer, 41.
Rule a Wife and have a Wife, 242—265.
———————————————— action of Hart and Mohun in it, 261.
———————————————— the merit of it, 262.
———————————————— Perez, a military coxcomb, *ibid.*
———————————————— Cacafogo, a bastard Falstaff, *ibid.*
———————————————— revived by Garrick, 263.
———————————————— passage explained, 265.
Ryan, 209, 210.
——— and Mrs. Younger inferior to Wilks and Mrs. Oldfield, 263.
——— his Macduff, 118.
Rymer's praise of Hart, 56.
——— opinion of Hart and Mohun, 130.

S.

Savage's poem of the Bastard, 173.
Scarron, 49.
Scene between Brutus and Cassius in Julius Cæsar, 159, *et seq.*
Scottish crown not hereditary, 78.
Sedley, 218.
Sejanus, by Ben Jonson, 14, 15.
——— inferior to Shakspeare's third-rate tragedies, 54.

Sejanus,

Sejanus, the author's own account of its ill succefs, 54.
Seymour, (Mrs.) 179.
Shakspeare's creative powers, 4.
——————— superior knowledge of human nature, 13, 14.
——————— uses merriment in his most serious plays, 13, 14.
——————— and Ben Jonson, 35, 36, &c. &c.
——————— an actor, 35, 53.
——————— his use of vulgar errors, 71.
——————— not very exact in the choice of words, 96, 223, 224.
——————— his predilection for Brutus, 128.
——————— his character of Cæsar, 128, 129.
——————— unjustly criticised, 134.
——————— his characters superior to all others, 207.
——————— a moralist, 205, 210.
——————— his female characters, 237.
——————— his first play, 252.
——————— his style imitated by Beaumont and Fletcher, 253.
——————— his power over his auditors, 255.
——————— one of the audience, 259.
Shepherd, 66.
Shirly and Cibber, 4.
Shuter, 41.
Sickness, a poem, by Mr. W. Thomson, 77.
Silent Woman, 63.
——————— revived in 1752, 63; with little succefs, *ibid.*
——————— sonnet in the first act, 64.
Smith, Palmer, Dodd, and Baddeley, commenced, 45.
——— (Wm.) 153, 209.
Soliloquy of Sejanus, 55.
Sophocles, 214.
Southern, 200, 224.
Sparks, 188.
——— his death, and dying-request, *ibid.*

Speech

Speech of Macbeth to the prefiding hag, 112; compared with the dame's invocation from Jonſon, 113, 114.
Spelman, 125.
Steevens, 16, 20, 21, 23, 32, 75, 76, 89, 97, 99, 102, &c.
——, Warburton, and Vanini, 174.
Stone, (Miſs.) her hiſtory, 214, 216.
Suetonius, 139.
Suidas, 221.
Superſtition of the actors, 6.
Swift, 8.
Sylla, 149.

T.

Tate, 168, 170, 171.
—— his ſcenes of Edgar and Cordelia in Lear, 169.
Taylor, 63, 208.
Thane, explained, 125, 126.
Theobald, 16.
—— defended, 21, 22.
Thomſon, Mr. W. 77.
Tiberius and Macro, 55.
Tollet, 230.
Tooke, (Horne,) 188.
Tragedy without female characters, 132
Tribunes at Rome, 149.
Tricks of old impoſtors, 189.
Triumvirate at Rome, 149.
Twelfth-Night, 237.
Two noble Kinſmen, 401.
Tyrwhit, 16, 21.

V.

Valerio and Evanthe, 257, 258.
Vaughan, Mrs. Pritchard's brother, 42, 43.
Victor's Hiſtory of the Stage, 141.

Underhill,

INDEX.

Underhill, 153.
Volpone, fable of, 60.
———— the last act censured, 61.
———— actors in it, 61, 62.
Voltaire's Mort de Cæsar, 132, 133.

W.

Walker, 211.
Warburton, 9, 136, 175, 191, 192, 199.
———— and Steevens, 75, 94, 97, 198, 201, 204, 222, &c. &c.
Ward, (Mrs.) Delane, and Garrick, 44, 45.
———— her Dame Kitely, 42.
———— her death, 44.
Wardship, abuse of, 6, 7.
Warton, 97.
Weston, 67.
Wife for a Month, 256.
———————— its plot and manners described at large, 256, 257.
Wilks, 61, 81, 124, 209, 241.
——— his action in Antony, 155.
——— his defects, 157.
Wilks, Mrs. Booth, and Boheme, 178, 179.
William the Conqueror, 196.
Williams, 153.
Winston, 42, 137.
———— Bransby, and Sparks, in the part of Kent, 188.
Winter's Tale, 260.
Witchcraft, 70.
———— modern stage-witches, 74.
———— royal, banished, 116.
Woffington, (Mrs.) 4, 5.
Woodward, 6, 26, 41, 172, 263.
———— and Garrick, 43, 44.
———— and Mrs. Pritchard, 263, 264.

Y Yates,

Y.

Yates, 41, 67.
—— (Mrs.) 240, 251.

END of INDEX to VOL. II.

www.ingramcontent.com/pod-product-compliance
Lightning Source LLC
Chambersburg PA
CBHW031340230426
43670CB00006B/394